OUR FATHER, WHO ART ON EARTH

The Lord's Prayer for
Believers and **Unbelievers**

JOSÉ TOLENTINO MENDONÇA
FOREWORD BY ENZO BIANCHI

Paulist Press
Mahwah, NJ / New York

Cover image by Pokaz/Shutterstock.com
Cover design by Sharyn Banks
Book design by Lynn Else

Originally published in Portugal as *Pai-Nosso que estais na Terra, O Pai-Nosso aberto a crentes e a não-crentes*
© 2011, INSTITUTO MISSIONÁRIO FILHAS DE SÃO PAULO – PAULINAS EDITORA
    Rua Francisco Salgado Zenha, 11 – 2685-332 Prior Velho – Portugal
    www.paulinas
English translation by Mary John Ronayne, OP, copyright © 2012 by Paulinas Editora

Library of Congress Cataloging-in-Publication Data

Mendonça, José Tolentino.
    [Pai-Nosso que estais na terra. English]
    Our Father, who art on earth : the Our Father for believers and unbelievers / José Tolentino Mendonça ; foreword by Enzo Bianchi. - English-language ed.
       p. cm.
    ISBN 978-0-8091-4798-4 (alk. paper) - ISBN 978-1-58768-238-4
    1. Lord's prayer—Criticism, interpretation, etc. I. Title.
    BV230.M4613 2013
    226.9'606-dc23

                                      2012042274

ISBN: 978-0-8091-4798-4 (paperback)
ISBN: 978-1-58768-238-4 (e-book)

Published in North America by Paulist Press in 2013
997 Macarthur Boulevard
Mahwah, New Jersey 07430

www.paulistpress.com

Printed and bound in the
United States of America

Water, is taught by thirst.

Emily Dickinson

CONTENTS

Foreword by Enzo Bianchi vii

Prologue xiii

CHAPTER 1: The Cry 1

CHAPTER 2: Is God in Paris? 9

CHAPTER 3: The Evaporation of the Father 19

CHAPTER 4: A Father Who Becomes Our Father 27

CHAPTER 5: Where Are You? 35

CHAPTER 6: To Give a Name without Losing What
              Cannot Be Said 43

CHAPTER 7: Learning to Live According to God's Will 55

CHAPTER 8: We Still Have a Childhood to Live 63

CHAPTER 9: Our Lives Are Fed on a Life Shared 73

CHAPTER 10: God Has Faith in Us 81

CHAPTER 11: A Unilateral Decision to Love 89

CHAPTER 12: The Fourth Temptation 97

CHAPTER 13: The Wound Bears Fruit 105

FOREWORD
Enzo Bianchi
Prior of Bose Monastery

In this book, José Tolentino Mendonça faces a brave and difficult
challenge: addressing both believers and unbelievers in the
words of the *Our Father*, the Christian prayer par excellence, the
prayer described by Tertullian as the "epitome of the whole
gospel." The author finds in the *Our Father* a light for the human
being as such, a set of footprints indicating a pathway open to
men and women as human beings, preceding even their beliefs
and confessional allegiances.

The idea that makes this undertaking possible is that this
prayer expresses the humanity of human beings, so much so that
every person can find him/herself represented in the *Our Father*.
The author's decision to address himself also to unbelievers is no
mere worldly concession. Rather, it springs from the conviction
of a mature faith that Jesus is "master of humanity," that the
human mirrors the divine, that men and women are images of
God and that everything that is human concerns God. This
openness to the other, even to those who do not, cannot, or do
not know how to believe, produces an effect of essentiality and
simplicity in the author's outlook, an outlook that he makes full
use of in the vision of life and of the Christian faith presented in
this book. He reflects on the universal dimension of the *Our*

Father: this universality has to do with the fact that men and women, sons and daughters, every single person has an inner life, is a being of desire, needing bread and forgiveness, struggling with evil, living in that land which, thanks to the Incarnation, is no longer a place that separates people from God, but is the only place where an encounter between the human being and God is possible.

This commentary, which does not follow the usual and often repetitive lines of so many exegetical or spiritual texts on the *Our Father*, reveals its originality above all in the high quality of the language used. It is couched in a literary style that also reveals the author's poetic gift. And the lovely phrase of Emily Dickinson's ("Water, is taught by thirst"), which is used as an epigraph, gives the reader a clue to the kind of path that lies ahead. The poetic word, that word which alone is capable of bearing the weight of being, is the one that best echoes the simple and inexhaustible words of the *Our Father*.

Then there are the many references, chiefly to literary sources, because faith is the telling of a story and literature is a teacher of life, the transmission of human wisdom through the telling of a story. The references, which are never heavy or ends in themselves, are also philosophical and psychoanalytical, because the human effort to understand the human being is part of the toil that we must undertake under the sun, as we are reminded by Qoheleth. Nevertheless, above all, the decisive and fundamental reference is to the word of the Bible. Cross references to various biblical passages become a kind of dance in the Biblical text in which the reader is invited to join, moving from Genesis to Revelation, from the Gospel according to Saint Luke to that according to John, from Matthew to the Letter to the Hebrews. An exegete's familiarity with the Bible, as well as the passionate faith of a lover of the Scriptures accustomed to *lectio divina*, make the commentary a real symphony in which the

Word of God is attuned to human words and calls on us to make of Christian life a life lived poetically. Or, if we prefer, a dance led by the great dancer of the eschatological dance, Jesus Christ. Commenting on the petition for our daily bread, the author begins the dance with the invitation:

> Let us feed one another. We are here for one another, whether listening or speaking, in silence or in laughter, in giving and in loving, a necessary food, because our lives are nourished with life (and a life that is shared).

In addition to its breadth of spirit, his clear desire to remain within the spirit of the Second Vatican Council, and his love for people, what seems to me personally most important in Tolentino's book is the way in which he enters fully into what I consider to be, today, a task that the Church is called on to carry out, namely, the task of helping to reconstruct a grammar of the human. Faced with textures of family and social life that are unraveling, with the way in which the inhuman is invading our daily lives, with the fact that the economic predominates over the educational, the Church, disciple of Christ, "Master of humanity" who came "to teach us how to live our lives in this world" (Titus 2:12), is called on, together with all men and women of good will, to share in the reconstruction of the meaning of words, gestures, and relationships that make human experience beautiful and livable. They make it a reflection of the beauty that came forth from the hands of God the Creator. And so it is that trust and forgiveness, waiting and hope, fraternity and desire, beauty and thirst and all the other human realities implied in the *Our Father*, become expressions of the man or woman who is endeavoring to make of his or her life a masterpiece of holiness; in other words, of all those who are endeavoring to become human according to the image of the humanity of

God as both portrayed and lived by Jesus Christ. According to the patristic teaching on the Incarnation, God in Christ lived the experience of being a human being within himself, making man's otherness come about within himself. Hippolytus of Rome wrote: "We know that the Word became man, of the same clay as ourselves (man as we ourselves are men)." Jesus of Nazareth portrayed God within the confines of a human being, he gave our human senses to God, thereby enabling God to experience the world and human otherness, and the world and human beings to experience the otherness of God. *Bodiliness* is the essential place for this portrayal that makes the humanity of Jesus of Nazareth the primordial sacrament of God. Jesus' language and, in particular, his word, but also his senses, his emotions, his gestures, the way he greeted people and looked at them, his words filled with tenderness and his prophetic utterances, his patient instruction and sharp reproof of the disciples, his weariness and his strength, his weakness and his tears, his joy and his exultation, the silences and withdrawals into solitude, his relationships and his encounters, his freedom and his courage are all flashes of Jesus' humanity, which the Gospels allow us to glimpse through the revealing but opaque window of the written word. They constitute luminous reflections that enable us to contemplate something of the divine light. The otherness and transcendence of God are proclaimed by Jesus and translated into human practice and language in the intimacy of ordinary everyday life…God is the *Abba*, daddy, father, dad, "pop."

It is the living out of the humanity of Jesus that proclaims God and opens for us a way that leads us to Him. "No one has ever seen God. It is God the only Son…who has made him known [*exeghésato*]" (John 1:18). The verb *exeghéomai* conveys both the meaning of "to explain," "to expound the exegesis," "to narrate," and also the idea of "pointing towards," "leading [someone] to." Central to this journey towards the Father, in which we become Christians by becoming human, is the prayer of the *Our Father*, in which we enter into a filial relationship with God both as brothers and sisters of Jesus Christ and, in him, with all other human beings. In fact, as our author reminds us in the words of Saint Augustine, "Jesus wanted us to address his own Father as our Father too."

PROLOGUE

There is a song by Jacques Prévert that begins with the words "Our Father who art in heaven. Stay there, and we'll stay on earth." Where is God? And where are we? Irony is, at times, the fragile form we have for hiding this kind of nowhere in which we live our lives, between fire and ashes, between helplessness and presence, between cry and prayer. But it also happens that the impasse not only gives back the measure of the distance but, mysteriously, reveals to us the unexpected closeness. The earth, this earth that is daily kneaded with convulsion and desire, is what separates us from or brings us close to God.

THE CRY

"When You Pray..."

Keep a place in your heart for the unexpected guest.
Henri Frédéric Amiel

When springtime comes, nature seems to overcome the stillness
of winter and to multiply the almost imperceptible signs of its
rebirth. There is a sap that revitalizes the landscape of the world.
Even in the wastelands, in the empty yards and uninhabited
properties, in the least cultivated gardens, spring appears with
amazing energy. At the same time, this rebirth of the world
sometimes seems to us incomparably simpler than our own. We
ourselves tend to feel buried and lifeless. We think that too much
time has already passed, that at some point in our journey we got
lost, and that this is perhaps something that cannot now be put
right. We are inclined to get bogged down in an unspoken con-
formism, dissatisfied and procrastinating to the point of giving
up altogether. The call to renewal certainly does not leave us
indifferent; it must always startle us. But we view it more with
nostalgia than with hope. We contemplate it at a distance,
shielded by countless excuses. We do our best to defend ourselves, pretending that we do not perceive. Deep within ourselves, we feel that spring is not now for us. But, in our hearts,
we find ourselves facing the question recorded in the Gospel, a
question that gives us no peace until we have answered it: "How

can anyone be born after having grown old? Can one enter a second time into the mother's womb and be born?" (John 3:4).

WE PASS THROUGH OUR OWN HOUSE LIKE STRANGERS

I am reminded of Sophia de Mello Breyner Andresen's short story entitled "Silence." It begins with a description of the peace that envelops us, us and things; the peace that, at times, is so obvious that we take it for granted; the peace we experience as a comfort zone, like a habit, a well-known landscape, a matter of routine. Everything, inside and around us, even though requiring effort, presents no surprises, is as it should be, in its proper place. And if we do acknowledge the effort entailed, we feel that it also consoles us and reassures us: "Her hands had become rough, she was tired of being on her feet and her back was aching. But interiorly, she felt a great cleanliness as if, instead of having been washing the dishes, she had been washing her soul. The unshaded light in the kitchen was causing the white tiles to shine. Outside, in the mild summer night, a cypress tree was gently swaying....And Joanna slowly passed through the house....A quiet silence hovered everywhere like a prolonged thirst. Touching the white wall with her hands, Joanna drew a quiet breath. All this was her kingdom."

We can look upon the sphere of life in which we move, with its fixed outlines, its rhythms, its clearly defined spaces, as if it were an unassailable kingdom, our own kingdom. We feel we are safe. For much of the time, the vision we have of our lives is that of a comfortable territory, free of surprises, without any great questionings or oscillations, to such an extent that we identify ourselves, we cling to this vision. But sooner or later, we find ourselves being challenged to recognize that this is only a part; it is not the whole.

Sophia de Mello Breyner Andresen's story goes on as follows: at precisely the moment in which everything seemed to her to be in order, Joanna heard a cry and did not quite know where it had come from. At first she thought that it might be out in the street on the other side of her house. In fact, she seemed to be hearing the voice of a woman "a shrill, wild, solitary voice," a voice that had been restrained and was now making itself heard, an ancient, unknown voice that had been silent for many years. What could that be? She did not understand. But suddenly things became more complex. She felt she was losing her foothold, pierced through by that cry, as if it had penetrated her flesh, had come indeed from within herself, had come from far away in her life and she was no longer the same person. She looked around and "everything had become an absurd accident, disconnected, no longer a kingdom. The things were no longer hers, they were no longer her, nor were they part of her. Everything had become alien…." For the first time, in a mixture of pain and fear, "she walked through her house like a stranger."

MAKING GOOD USE OF CRISES

The term *crisis* has become trivialized to such an extent that it is perhaps a bit risky to continue using it in order to describe the construction of one's inner, spiritual itinerary, the slow and contradictory growth to maturity that is ours. Nevertheless, at a time when there is a shortage of masters, and we seem to be committed to a distracted kind of self-management (when it is not a consuming isolation), such experiences "are in fact great masters that have something to teach us." To walk through our own lives like a stranger is not necessarily a bad thing. It allows us to look in a way we had not managed to do up to that point; it enables us to listen not only to life on the surface, but to our sense of dissatisfaction, our thirst for truth, and so begin to become pilgrims. Not to listen to ourselves in depth is to waste a precious opportunity of attaining that depth which can give a meaning to existence, even when we know that experiences such as these can be severe masters teaching us things that we rarely deem ourselves ready to learn....Perhaps we need to learn that, as we make our way through life, the great cycles of questioning, the intensification of the search, the times of impasse, the experiences of crises come about in order to escape a worse fate. And what might that worse fate be? Jesus of Nazareth tells us the answer: the worse fate is to have looked without actually seeing, to have listened without really hearing, to have perceived to some extent without really having taken things in. The worse fate is for us to recognize in ourselves the "lost opportunity" that the Gospel complains of (even though the dominant culture does all it can to make it seem normal and painless): "We played the flute for you, and you did not dance; we wailed, and you did not weep" (Luke 7:32).

It is not any of the deprivations, difficulties, and conflicts we may encounter that can rob us of our intense love of life. We need to widen or alter our perspective. I am reminded of the lines written by Etty Hillesum in a concentration camp: "O God, times are too hard for frail people like myself. I know that a new and kinder day will come. I would so much like to live on, if only to express all the love I carry within me in spite of everything that I encounter from day to day. And there is only one way of preparing the new age, by living it even now in our hearts. Somewhere in me I feel so light, without the least bitterness and so full of strength and love. I would so much like to go on living in order to help prepare the new age which will certainly come— do I not feel it already growing inside me from day to day?"

AN INITIATION INTO THE SPIRITUAL LIFE

One of the most enigmatic and at the same time most illuminating phrases in the Gospel is the one uttered by John the Baptist when he saw Jesus passing by. Turning to his disciples, the Baptist said: "Among you stands one whom you do not know" (John 1:26). I think that this phrase can be reformulated as follows: In our very midst, in the mysterious center of our relationship with God, with the world and with others, in the very center of the more or less free-flowing, or troubled, way we conduct our lives, there stands the One whom we do not know. Perhaps, in that deep-down, solitary and personal nugget of truth within us, there is a presence, a treasure, a wellspring that has yet to be discovered, a work of relationship, spiritual and vital, that has yet to be broached....The writer Christiane Singer has described a curious explanation that an anthropologist friend of hers told her he had heard given by an African tribesman: "No, sir, we do not have crises, we have initiations." The process of initiation is fundamental in the Christian liturgy and the administration of the sacraments. But there is also a road to be travelled when it comes to inserting this vital horizon into our day-to-day lives. This process of initiation is missing in our lives, in the normal course of our meetings and failures to meet, of our flashes of insight and our defeats. The days are not only a motley cavalcade that makes us dizzy. We need a connecting thread, we need a track to lead us to the meaning.

THE WISDOM OF LEARNING TO HOPE FOR NOTHING

The story is told of a disciple who went to his master for his first lesson. As it was the first time the two had met, the master cordially offered his new disciple a cup of tea. The young man held up his cup for the tea being poured by the master from the pot. Except that the master went on pouring, and pouring, until the cup was full, and still he went on pouring….The poor disciple, overcoming his shyness, said to him: "Master, Master, it's brimming over!" The Master replied: "This is the first lesson. If you do not hold your cup ready, everything you are going to receive will be wasted."

Let our spiritual experience not be like a heaping up of things and ideas, of programs….Let us not be in a hurry to fill the cup. It is much more valuable when it is empty. The important thing is just to be. There are no recipes for experiencing God. Each encounter is unique. What really matters is for us to feel ourselves part of this love story that the Lord wishes to live with us. He knows how to put right what is wrong, to find what has been lost, to revive the flame that is just about to die out….The Lord knows how to remake covenants with infinite patience.

One of the most fruitful ways of embarking on the inner journey is contained in the advice given by some monks: "Choose your place in the middle of a forest and withdraw to that place every day. And pray like this: 'Lord, I am here waiting for nothing….Lord, I am here waiting for nothing.'"

THE ART OF LISTENING

A time comes when we realize more clearly that life, like the earth, has geological layers; that life expands due to times of formation that are not visible on the surface; and that, in all existences, there is an earthly crust and meters and meters of filaments, all mixed together in silence. Unlike hastily formed judgments in which everything is smooth running, we have to acknowledge that the instruments we have with which to reach the hearts of others, and indeed our own heart, are disturbingly limited. Listening is perhaps the most suitable sense of verification with which to perceive the complexity of a life. But we so rarely listen to one another. In the Rule of Saint Benedict there is an expression that calls for an attentive listening: "Incline the ear of your heart." In other words, listening is not done only with the outer ear, nor is it merely to take in what is being said. Above all, it is an attitude, it is to incline oneself toward, it is to concentrate our attention, our readiness to take something in. To listen and to be listened to in depth and to the end opens, in the Spirit, wider horizons than those that we would be able to attain on our own and sets us once more on the path of hope.

One of the most impressive texts on the unquenchable need to listen is the short story entitled "Misery" by Anton Chekhov. It is the story of a sleigh driver, Iona, whose son has died and who can find no one ready to comfort him. "He wants to tell how his son was taken ill, how he suffered, what he said before he died, how he died....He wants to describe the funeral, and how he went to the hospital to get his son's clothes. He still has his daughter Anisya in the country....And he wants to talk about her too...," but no one will listen to him. The sleigh driver turns to his horse and while he is giving it its hay, he begins to tell it, in a heartbroken monologue, everything that has happened. The story ends as follows: "The little mare munches, listens, and breathes on her master's hands. Iona is carried away and tells her all about it."

What about ourselves? To whom will we tell our story?

2

IS GOD IN PARIS?

"Pray Thus…"

I do not know who first taught us to pray and how we cope with prayer today. Almost certainly, we all have different ways of praying. For some of us, perhaps our way of praying is embedded in our earliest childhood memories. We learned how to pray when we were enfolded in that primordial world peopled by key figures such as our parents or a grandmother, with its rhythms, its smells, the comforting background of conversations without beginning or end. Others of us, however, may have come to prayer on our own, as adults, as if making a U-turn, maybe even going against our family's customs. Either we have prayed since we became aware of ourselves, or we have only just begun to pray. Prayer either punctuates our daily round like a kind of living and undulating breathing, or prayer does not occupy much space in our lives, nor do we yet fully realize the need for it, except on certain sporadic occasions of which we have no clear picture.

The poet Rainer Maria Rilke helps us in our search for a meaning. He wrote: "Things aren't all so tangible and sayable as people would usually have us believe; most experiences are unsayable, they happen in a space that no word has ever entered." The biography of our prayer is along these lines. It retains an element that is unsayable. Even if in fact spelled out, there remains a secret thread, an unfinished story. Those who pray perceive better than anyone else the doubts, the difficulties, the hiatuses that can surround the path of prayer, since prayer is a never-ending apprenticeship.

WE PRAY BECAUSE WE *ARE* A PRAYER

The key word is *relationship*. In order to understand what prayer is, even before looking at the specific legacy of the religious picture, we need to examine the anthropological structure of which we are all made. The secret is this: we are a prayer. At our root, at the bottom of what, in us, is being and language, there is a fundamental experience that separates us absolutely from solitude or self-sufficiency. None of us is the origin of him- or herself (in the terminology of the Scholastics, human beings are not *ens causa sui*). We do not make ourselves, to begin with, now, or at any time in the future. We come from a horizon and circumstances that transcend us. It is true that the possibility is always open to us of shaping in a particular way what we have received from the Other, but our interiority, our own intimacy, our way forward is always in a creative and indispensable encounter between the "I" and the "Thou."

We only need to think about what happens with language. There are two theories about the origin of language that, in effect, are taken for granted. We could define one of these as "communicative" (the idea being that we speak in order to transfer our thoughts from one mind to another), and the other as "cognitive" (the idea in this case being that we speak in order to articulate our own thinking more clearly). Both these theses regard language as a mental reality, that is, a given that has more to do with thought than with the body, more with the process of reasoning than with the exchange of emotions. But there is a book by the anthropologist Dean Falk, *Finding Our Tongues: Mothers, Infants and the*

Origin of Language, in which she suggests, on the contrary, that each of us begins to use linguistic sounds, not so much to communicate or to think, but in order to remain in touch with those who are caring for us. Words are the verbalization of the desire that we feel for the other in us. In essence, whatever it is that we want to say, we say it in order to bring, or to keep, the other close to us, to delay or deny their absence, to say how much they mean to us. Hence, human language is an astonishing consequence of our need for relationship. What is prayer if not just this: *life's fragile and incomplete construction of relationship?* In prayer, God moves from the third to the second person. He ceases to be a "He" or an "It" in order to become, for us, a "Thou." He ceases to be vague and indefinite and assumes the possibility, the proximity, of a Face. Prayer is a mother tongue.

THE ORIGINALITY OF JESUS OF NAZARETH

At the time of Jesus, there were different currents within Judaism or, to put it in today's terms, there were various Judaisms. For example, we hear of Pharisees, Sadducees, Essenes, the group around John the Baptist. It was by prayer that each of these groups was identified. It was prayer that bound the members of each group together spiritually and sociologically, and that was a means of attaching group labels, approximating, making distinctions. Even the prayers common to all could give rise to differentiating forms and intensities. The Gospel records that one day as Jesus was praying, one of the disciples approached him and said: "Lord, teach us to pray as John taught his disciples" (Luke 11:1).

We have no idea what it must have been like to see Jesus praying! What the disciples saw must have been an extraordinary spectacle of intimacy and trust, and, understandably, they asked to be initiated into this experience. But this move forward happened when the process of discipleship had already become a clear central fact, different from everything they knew. Jesus was leading them into unfamiliar territory and needed a form of prayer capable of expressing this. Hence, the brief request "Lord, teach us to pray" conceals a long period of growth and discovery.

The disciples' request is not entirely new. In a sense, the novelty is on Jesus' part. "Pray then in this way: 'Our Father, who art in heaven, hallowed be thy name; thy kingdom come, thy will be done on earth as it is in heaven. Give us this day our daily bread; forgive us our trespasses as we forgive those who trespass against us; and lead us not into temptation, but deliver us from evil'" (cf. Matt 6:9–13). As Tertullian wrote around the beginning of the third century, the brevity of this prayer "contains a great and luminous meaning, and in proportion as it is restrained in wording, so does it expand in our hearts."

WHAT IS A FATHER?

In order to understand the *Our Father* (and I would venture to say all Christian prayer), we need to discover the meaning of this "Father" whom we address. What is a father? My father is both outside and inside me. He is a person of flesh and blood, who has a history, a way of being, a temperament, who maintained with me a series of fundamental relationships. But a father is also within, inside each one of us. He is the one that we refer to as *imago*, in other words, a kind of psychic representation that gives us a model to cement our inner architecture. In fact, in order to be able to grow, to acquire the necessary self-confidence, we all needed to have our father inside us, and not merely outside. In fact, we incorporated him. Later on, we projected ourselves onto him, we sought to imitate him, to be like him, to grow to his stature that already to us seemed incalculable, to acquire his strength and ability that we already took to be absolute and protective.

The grammar of life, in all its singularity, requires of us some form of incorporation of both mother and father. Their image is not only something that we see in front of us, but something that develops inside us. This "gestation" enables the child to develop interiorly and make progress in the confidence that will be the art of a life. In one of his books, the psychoanalyst João dos Santos tells an interesting story. The children in the Casa da Praia, an institute that he founded, were brought together for a game in which they were to launch an assault on a castle. The teachers had prepared everything and the whole class was about to assault the castle, in full daylight, with swords and helmets made of cardboard. The game was more or less like the kind we ourselves used to play as children. But just as the battle was about to begin, one little four-year-old refused to take part. When he was urged to pluck up courage, he began to cry, saying: "I'm afraid. I have no strength. I can't fight a battle, my father is in Paris." None of the other children's parents were there present so that the whereabouts of that particular father should not have mattered. But what the child was trying to say was at another level. What was really happening was that the child was struggling with this idea: "The image of my father is not yet sufficiently strong inside me for me to be able to fight without having him beside me. My father is a long way off, and for this reason I am much more fragile than the others, I do not feel able to take the risk....What I need is for his presence to be sufficiently stable and luminous inside me."

Think back to when we were children and were too shy to look at strangers. Without either our father or our mother nearby, we did not move a step, we needed them to cling to, we fed on their closeness. It is rather paradoxical, but that is how things are. We only begin to become independent in relation to our parents when they begin to be securely installed inside us. This is what was missing for the little boy in the story. The absence of his father within him, as it were, paralyzed him.

If we wish to get to know a man or a woman, we shall have to discover toward whom it is that their lives are secretly orientated. They continue to converse with the person they are happiest conversing with, even when they are apparently conversing with others. It all depends on who it is they have chosen as father. It all depends on with whom they communicate in silence, for whose benefit have they accumulated deeds and proofs, for love of whom have they made what they have made of their lives. For most people, there will never have been more than one such interlocutor: either father or mother. Figures that reign supreme, either through their presence or their absence, releasing or crushing life with all the weight of what they did not know how to be or to give. "Look what I'm doing! I'm doing it for you, to win your love, to make you turn your eyes in my direction, so that, with the full light of your eyes, you will give me the certainty, the assurance that I deserve to exist."

Many of us are under a shadow, enclosed in our father's garden, our mother's room, and to the end of our lives we continue to address our appeals to someone who is not there. The secret reason for what we do, even when we appear to be very positive and free, continues to be a confrontation, a settling of accounts or else an irrepressible desire to please. How many people, especially in the most extreme cases, commit acts of unwarranted violence because, deep down, they did not feel sufficiently loved by either father or mother! Violence is a cry for help. It must be seen as a bizarre request for love: "Love me, redeem my past." But even in our ordinary and (more) peaceful lives, it is not unusual for this to be still a secret cause of suffering.

In short, the question of the father as an inner model is the question of the stability of our inner life. In fact, we are always arranging various "fathers" for ourselves. We set up forms of defense against their absence that are extremely symptomatic. For example, when we are away from our habitual world, at a distance from our normal comfort zone, we begin to look around at the crowd of strangers and, all of a sudden, we seem to recognize someone. We encounter someone who reminds us physically of a member of our family, a distant cousin, a friend, a neighbor. Evidently such resemblances do exist, but we pay greater attention to them (or we may even invent them) when we need to, when the context leaves us feeling somewhat insecure and deprived of affective anchors. We need these resemblances in order to acquire a certain degree of security. The truth is that we are always searching for someone. We are ever on the lookout for a "father."

There are people who believe that they are totally independent of an "inner father," but in fact they are not. We all know people who are capable of going fearlessly and unaccompanied to the North Pole or to Timbuktu, but afterward, they can never face their inner life on their own for a single second. Interior objects are not fixed and settled. They are shot through with a lack of satisfaction, which is reflected, at times, in an extraordinary desire to consume, to buy, to move from place to place, to talk incessantly, to undertake too many overlapping commitments. The drive to consume (goods, experiences, sentiments) may well be a disguised need for a "father." The underlying reason is the inability to abide by Jesus' recommendation: "But whenever you pray, go into your room and shut the door and pray to your Father who is in secret; and your Father who sees in secret will reward you" (Matt 6:6).

At times we notice, rather sadly, that even centers of pilgrimage very soon turn rather grotesquely into islands surrounded by all-consuming commercialism. Think of Fatima, Lourdes, Jerusalem. It is easier to settle for a superficial emotion and then fill the vacuum, bridge over the gap, attenuate the fact of not having, in fact, found God as Father. It is the anxiety generated by this absence that feeds the consumerist frenzy. Why? We are moving about all the time with the "father," in search of a "father," and we have to be aware of this. If we do not have the humility and the honesty to tread a fully conscious path, alternative routes will multiply surreptitiously.

A very important moment in the spiritual journey of Francis of Assisi occurred when, in order to acknowledge his vocation in the face of the opposition of his family, he stripped off his clothes before his father (clothes that belonged to his father, clothes that "were" his father). By this gesture, Francis "stripped himself" of that father and his intransigence. By thus stripping off his clothes, he said, even without words: "I want, I need another 'Father.' I don't want to be dependent only on the father of my childhood; I respect my father, but I cannot but keep moving toward God." In fact, our meeting with God as Father cannot come about without our experiencing (and accepting) our nakedness, the stripping off of the models that we have accumulated over time, so that God can at last become the inner fountain that waters our life.

At a given moment, it becomes abundantly clear that, in order to pray the *Our Father*, we have to welcome God, not just from time to time, but as an inner model, an abiding image, a presence with which we are in unceasing dialogue. To become the "image and likeness of God" is to have in God our inner skeleton, our root, our unequivocal foundation. How many times do we not say with the little four-year-old: "I can't manage it. I don't know how to. I can't, God is in Paris!"?

TAKE THE *OUR FATHER* SERIOUSLY

Simone Weil wrote that it is impossible to conceive of a prayer that is not already contained in the *Our Father*, which "is to prayer as Christ is to humanity." Moreover: "it is impossible to say it, once you are doing so and you are giving to each word your full attention, without a change, perhaps infinitesimal but real taking place in one's soul." We only reach the *Our Father* when we feel ourselves taken hold of, perplexed, turned upside down, reborn through Jesus, or when we realize existentially that before Jesus was one thing and with Jesus is something completely different. We have to move from an exterior spirituality, unduly dependent on the sociological framework and its practices, into another more interior one which will enable us to discover that God is Father, He is my Father, He is "our Father."

When did Jesus teach the *Our Father* to the disciples? When they were able to recognize Jesus as something completely new. Prayer is a consequence rather than a cause. It is the expression of a way of living rather than of a discovery. The *Our Father* is born of a long journey together. It is at the peak of a particular stage of growth to maturity that the *Our Father* is revealed. We too must pray the *Our Father* in all truth when we come to realize, not in the line of history and its froth, but deep down within ourselves, that Jesus Christ brings the novelty of God. It may well be that, this being so, we need to follow Fernando Pessoa's advice and "learn to unlearn." Unlearn the labyrinths, all the webs, the models that suffocate us and are of use only in making us postpone the indispensable encounter with ourselves. Jesus causes us to reach a new boundary in God and our humanity. It was precisely because he sensed this that one of the disciples said to Jesus: "Lord, teach us to pray."

3

THE EVAPORATION OF THE FATHER

"Father…"

"What is left of the Father?" The Italian psychoanalyst Massimo Recalcati asks this question and his reply is: "Not much." In order to describe the times we live in, he quotes one of Jacques Lacan's expressions: "the evaporation of the father." At times for a reason—but certainly for no *good* reason—our culture, in fact, has, perpetrated a systematic demolition of the father figure. The father has ceased to be a value marker by which to assess a meaning, a point of reference that enables us to define the frontier between good and evil, between life and death. To a much greater extent than formerly, nowadays we tend to live in permanent suspicion relative to what the father represents, or else submerged in an overwhelming state of sadness. This generalized state of symbolic orphanhood results, for example, in our accepting uncertainty as a condition for happiness, so much so that only uncertainty seems to us to be valid.

The father figure needs to be recovered. This comes about by overcoming the opposition that has been established between Law and Desire, as if these were opposing and irreconcilable poles. To start, we need to discover desire in ourselves, even in the very earliest stage of our infancy, expressed as a desire for a continuation of the prenatal situation in which we were just one thing fused, as it were, with the loved object (in this case the body of our mother). The father is the one who appears as a third, a stranger with the symbolic function of releasing us from this vague "attachment" to our mother's body, showing us a difficult but real love, consisting of differentiated identities, limits, and independence. To recover the father, however, implies that we accept that the Law is not a threat but a condition of desire itself, and of authentic desire. The basic separation that is effected symbolically by the father creates a need, but it is the need that enables us to wish for things, that enables us to be.

In the spiritual field, too, we are witnessing an "evaporation of the father." The yearning for spirituality that is marked to a considerable extent by what is referred to as the "return to religiosity," runs the risk of being a kind of emotional drifting in search of a comfort zone that gives everything and in fact demands nothing, a dilution of awareness into some fusional experience, all the more welcome to the extent that it has not been brought about by the subject undergoing the experience. There is no Christian experience that does not involve discovering the Father. Saint Paul writes: "For you did not receive a spirit of slavery to fall back into fear, but you have received a spirit of adoption. When we cry, 'Abba! Father!' it is that very Spirit bearing witness with our spirit that we are children of God" (Rom 8:15–16).

PURIFYING THE FATHER IMAGES

However, merely to reinstate fatherhood symbolically is not enough. If we want to enter into the turnaround that Jesus offers in coming to know God, we must also venture to purify critically some of the father images. Often, our difficulty in our relationship with God is the result of the ambiguities that the resonance of the father figure still arouses in us. For example, one of the classics of European literature is Franz Kafka's *Letter to My Father*. This little book mirrors the heartbreaking interior process in which Kafka lived. He grew up in the shadow of his father, but at the same time carrying this terrible knot: however hard he tried, he would never be able to meet his requirements. The beginning of the letter clearly states the drama that this evoked: "Dearest Father, You asked me recently why I maintain that I am afraid of you. As usual, I was unable to think of any answer to your question, partly for the very reason that I am afraid of you, and partly because an explanation of the grounds for this fear would mean going into far more details than I could even approximately keep in mind while talking. And if I now try to give you an answer in writing, it will still be very incomplete because, even in writing, this fear and its consequences hamper me in relation to you." Now, it is not unusual, even among Christians, to encounter representations of a god very like the unattainable and dissatisfied figure of Kafka's father. It seems that however much we do or however hard we try, we never secure a benevolent look from God for ourselves. Everything of ours is insufficient, imperfect, not worth mentioning. The Christian proclamation is not that of a god like this, intransigently distributing his love. No, it is the proclamation of a God rich in mercy. Saint John's first letter tells us: "In this is love, not that we loved God but that he loved us" (1 John 4:10).

Other father images are unduly influenced by the stereotypes of the surrounding culture and they result in creating distance and aridity. The writer António Alçada Batista tells this typical story in the first person:

> Once I was operated on and was alone in the hospital with my father. I was in great pain, from my toenails to the roots of my hair, and my father was by my side. I was already nineteen years old, but I longed for his human and fatherly hand, and I said to him:

Let me see your hand.
What for?
I need your hand.

He smiled and gave it to me, but immediately those strict macho and academic rules that prevent a nineteen-year-old son from holding the loving hand of his father started operating within him and he began to withdraw his hand until my own was still pleading, but all on its own.

"I need your hand." To know God as a father can only be a lived experience, deeply experimental, something felt that enables us to have a share in something absolute. I am reminded of the prayer that one of the characters in a novel by Clarice Lispector utters while kneeling beside her bed: "Comfort my soul, help me to feel that your hand is in mine....Grant that I may have love for myself, as otherwise I cannot feel that God loves me.... Amen." The Good News brought by Jesus forbids us to persist in abstract and intellectualized formulas. As the author of the Letter to the Hebrews writes: "God is not ashamed to be called [our] God" (Heb 11:16). But we have to rid ourselves of certain images in order to be with the Father.

TO LOSE ONESELF AND TO FIND ONESELF

There is a text in the Gospel of Saint Luke that seems to do no more than describe an incident that occurred during Jesus' childhood, but which, seen in this light, is much more than that. Let us have a look at the account of the incident:

Now every year his parents went to Jerusalem for the festival of the Passover. And when he was twelve years old, they went up as usual for the festival. When the festival was ended and they started to return, the boy Jesus stayed behind in Jerusalem, but his parents did not know it. Assuming that he was in the group of travelers, they went a day's journey. Then they started to look for him among their relatives and friends. When they did not find him, they returned to Jerusalem to search for him. After three days they found him in the temple, sitting among the teachers, listening to them and asking them questions. And all who heard him were amazed at his understanding and his answers. When his parents saw him they were astonished; and his mother said to him, "Child, why have you treated us like this? Look, your father and I have been searching for you in great anxiety." He said to them, "Why were you searching for me? Did you not know that I must be in my Father's house?" But they did not understand what he said to them. (Luke 2:41–50)

What the Gospel is telling us is not the story of a child who gets lost in the midst of a festival. It is true that when children begin to get lost (or want to lose themselves), this is already a sign of something about their growth toward independence. No, this Gospel story sends us back to what we were saying earlier, namely, that in order for us to love God, for us to be aware of the presence of God in ourselves, we have to allow God to invade us, to impregnate us, to become our inner framework. We have to allow God to be the model of our lives. Deep down, it is this that is happening with Jesus.

When he was twelve years old....In Judaism, when a boy reaches the age of twelve, this marks the moment when he ceases to be a child and begins to be treated as an effective member of the people. Jesus feels that a new cycle is beginning for him. He is, as it were, invaded by the image of God. It is odd that, after this episode, he does not remain in the Temple. He returns with his parents, and Saint Luke tells us that "he was obedient to them." The substitution of interior models, this passage from "my father" to "our Father" does not mean we are allowed to cease caring for our own parents, loving them as we ought to love them. It has nothing to do with this. It is, however, connected with the understanding that our interior architecture has its great reference in God. This change is fundamental if we are to perceive the meaning of the prayer that Jesus teaches us.

Our experiences of family life may have been negative or extraordinarily positive. We may have encountered difficulties or have been given only happiness. This is not of great importance, because anyone who suffers either the one or the other is called upon to leave father and mother in order to find this God who is Father, and find Him in the depths of oneself.

To leave father and mother does not merely mean to leave, symbolically, the human family that gave us life. It is to leave the entire social and cultural context that also contributed to our upbringing. For we are not, in fact, merely the fruit of two human beings; rather, we are the result of many things. We are the result of what others think of us, of how they see us or we ourselves feel they see us; of what others hope for from us, of the good things that we hear said. We are the result of the desires that we nurture, of what we feel is best, or that will bring us greater opportunities. We are the result of a wide range of factors with which we will always be surrounded. But there comes a time when we need to say: I do not want to be merely the fruit of my father ("my father" meaning all these things that we have mentioned). I want, now, to be the child of the "our Father" to whom Jesus teaches me to pray.

GATES THAT HAD BEEN CLOSED

Anyone who has had the good fortune to read one of the books by the American novelist J. D. Salinger has almost certainly come across the Glass family, a New York family with its origins in Judaism and Ireland to which Franny belongs as the youngest of seven children. In the short story entitled "Franny," she is twenty years of age, is at university, has a casual boyfriend, is supposed to be a member of a theater group, is involved in all sorts of activities, but at the same time she increasingly feels out of place, having no place in that world in relation to which she behaves as kind of non-conformist, but also confused, isolated, harassed. She is aware of a dance of phantoms all around her that disgusts her: the dance "of ego, ego, ego. My own and everybody else's." The lack of authenticity with which she had lived quite neutrally is beginning to stifle her. She cannot bear fatuous casualness and hypocrisy, which quickly become the same thing, and as quickly fall apart. The academic knowledge she is acquiring leaves her dissatisfied. As she remarked at this point: "Sometimes I think that knowledge—when it's knowledge for knowledge's sake, anyway—is the worst of all." To manage to realize all this is an extraordinary grace, but Franny, in her anguish, is unable to perceive it. Oddly enough, what provoked her crisis was a little green book that she always carried with her: *The Way of a Pilgrim*, a classic text of Christian spirituality on prayer and spiritual enlightenment. She seems not to be prepared to read this text. She wavers continually between skepticism and acceptance, between a practical nihilism and an emotional search for faith, and that little book calls unequivocally for a decision. She will have to open doors that were closed against her.

It was to open doors like this that Nicodemus went in search of Jesus:

Now there was a Pharisee named Nicodemus, a leader of the Jews. He came to Jesus by night and said to him, "Rabbi, we know that you are a teacher who has come from God; for no one can do these signs that you do apart from the presence of God." Jesus answered him, "Very truly, I tell you, no one can see the kingdom of God without being born from above." Nicodemus said to him, "How can anyone be born after having grown old? Can one enter a second time into the mother's womb and be born?" Jesus answered, "Very truly, I tell you, no one can enter the kingdom of God without being born of water and Spirit. What is born of the flesh is flesh, and what is born of the Spirit is spirit. Do not be astonished that I said to you, 'You must be born from above.'" (John 3:1–7)

Meister Eckhart used to say: "The way I see God is the same as the way God sees me: my looking and God's looking are one, a single vision, the same knowing of love."

4

A FATHER WHO BECOMES
OUR FATHER

"Our Father"

Marcel Proust wrote:

> There are certain spirits which we can compare to
> sick people whom a kind of laziness or frivolity pre-
> vents from penetrating spontaneously into the deeper
> regions of themselves, where the true life of the spirit
> begins. Only when they have been led to these depths
> will they be capable of discovering and exploring true
> riches. But unless they make this effort, they will con-
> tinue to live on the surface in a perpetual forgetful-
> ness of themselves, in a kind of passivity which
> makes of them the plaything of all pleasures, reduc-
> ing them to the stature of those who surround them
> and disturb them. And like the nobleman who, hav-
> ing shared, from childhood onwards, the life of high-
> waymen, no longer remembered his own name, as for
> a long time he had ceased to use it, they would end
> up doing away, within themselves, with every vestige
> and every remembrance of their spiritual nobility.
> Unless, of course, an exterior impulse inserts them
> once more into the life of the spirit.

We ourselves are often like that nobleman who, through having lived apart from his real self and never having fully entered into his own identity, ends up not quite knowing who he is. Only an intervention of the Spirit (and we would write Spirit with a capital *S*) can return him to his true center, to his most vital core, and whisper to him what he really is, through penetrating layers and layers of neglect. The *Our Father* can prove to be this disturbing factor. Origen used to say, quite rightly, that our life is an endless and unending *Our Father*. The challenge is to recognize this.

WHEN JESUS SAYS "OUR FATHER"

The *Our Father* ought to astonish us. We have become so accustomed to living with the *Our Father* that we risk not fully appreciating its meaning. As Oscar Wilde reminded us, repetition can become something very unspiritual. But the first people to hear Jesus say *Abba* felt quite the opposite because they realized that they were in the presence of something very extraordinary: there was Someone who actually called God "Father." Other people hearing this might well have considered this scandalous, an unacceptable way of praying. Why? Because it is easier to see God from a distance—great, transcendent, powerful, a liberator, but always from a distance. The turnaround that Jesus of Nazareth introduced was to look at God from within. Jesus presents himself as the Son of God. His relationship with God is a filial relationship. In other words, Jesus is telling us that God is within him to such an extent that he is Son and is aware of himself as such. Reflect on the intensity of the witness that Jesus gives:

> Philip said to him, "Lord, show us the Father, and we
> will be satisfied." Jesus said to him, "Have I been with

you all this time, Philip, and you still do not know me? Whoever has seen me has seen the Father. How can you say, 'Show us the Father'? Do you not believe that I am in the Father and the Father is in me? The words that I say to you I do not speak on my own; but the Father who dwells in me does his works. Believe me that I am in the Father and the Father is in me; but if you do not, then believe me because of the works themselves." (John 14:8–11)

It is not merely a special kind of knowledge that Jesus gives us of God. He is not a prophet, a lawmaker, an intermediary. It is something quite else: God is his *imago*, the extraordinary and intimate source that molds and illuminates the messianic creativity of his words and of his gestures. In a way, Jesus' program is this sonship, this filial meshing. Just as, many times, we do things without knowing quite why we do them—it is because of the father image that we carry within us and with which we converse. Now, Jesus does this with God Himself. Everything in him was marked by this awareness of his sonship. He really could call God "*Abba*," in just the way children address their fathers, calling them "Papa," "Dad," "Daddy," not through any childish dependence, but through a mature and well-tried practice of a filial relationship. When Jesus says, "Our Father," "Our *Abba*," he is saying that God is the God of all times, the One in whom one can place one's trust, as a child trusts in its father unreservedly, openly, totally, and absolutely. God is the One to whom we can say, "I need your hand," "Give me your hand," and know that He will give it, that He takes care, accompanies, protects, does everything for us. For me to say "*Abba*" implies that I, too, want to place myself in the presence of God with the simplicity of a child, that I want to become like the person who prays in the psalm:

O Lord, my heart is not lifted up,
  my eyes are not raised too high;
I do not occupy myself with things
  too great and too marvellous for me.
But I have calmed and quieted my soul,
  like a weaned child with its mother;
    my soul is like the weaned child that is with me.

(Psalm 131:1–2)

How much unrest, irritability, disorderliness comes from our not having the soul of a child filled with its Father, but allowing ourselves to become entangled in the labyrinth of unceasingly temporary and inadequate substitutions.

HE WANTED US TO CALL HIS OWN FATHER "OUR FATHER"

Baptism does not make us followers, supporters, servants, or soldiers of Jesus. Neither does it cause us merely to discover in Jesus an extraordinary personality who has made an abiding mark in history, making of us merely spectators spellbound by admiration in relation to him. To use one of the loveliest expressions in the New Testament, which occurs in the Letter to the Hebrews, we can say that Baptism makes us companions of Jesus Christ ("For we have become partners of Christ" [Heb 3:14]).

Why companions? To cite the Letter to the Hebrews once again: we are his companions because he was not ashamed to call us brothers and sisters (He "…is not ashamed to call them brothers and sisters, saying, 'I will proclaim your name to my brothers and sisters, in the midst of the congregation I will praise you'" [Heb 2:11–12]). When speaking about God, Jesus never used the words *our Father*. He did indeed frequently speak of God as "my Father," or even "the heavenly Father." But when he

taught the *Our Father* to his disciples, Jesus said "Our Father," as
if he wished to explain the mystery of communion that unites us
in him. When we pray the *Our Father*, we really are partakers in
Christ. His being, his way, his style become ours, because "his
Father" is "our Father." In other words, he shares with us his vital
and interior architecture, his interior framework, the One towards
whom he turns continually. The Prologue to Saint John's Gospel
tells us: "But to all who received him, who believed in his name,
he gave power to become children of God" (John 1:12). And as
Saint Augustine wrote in his commentary on the *Our Father*:
"Jesus wanted us to call his Father our Father." In fact, Jesus does
not give us formulas; he leads us into an existential and practical relationship; he gives us access to a filial relationship. Jesus
does not give us knowledge of something. He gives us a taste of
God. Something to relish.

Seen in this light, we understand more clearly some fundamental passages in the writings of Saint Paul. First, in the Letter
to the Romans:

> For all who are led by the Spirit of God are children
> of God. For you did not receive a spirit of slavery to
> fall back into fear, but you have received a spirit of
> adoption. When we cry, "Abba! Father!" it is that very
> Spirit bearing witness with our spirit that we are chil-
> dren of God, and if children, then heirs, heirs of God
> and joint heirs with Christ—if, in fact, we suffer with
> him so that we may also be glorified with him. (Rom
> 8:14–17)

This first step enables us to perceive how to move on from
"my father" to "our Father." This progression is a consequence of
Easter. Plunged into the Passover of Jesus, we are called to live of
his Spirit, molded in accordance with his reality. We do not continue to be servants or slaves, but become in fact sons and

daughters of God, and we behave as such in the world ("You shine like stars in the world," declares the Letter to the Philippians [2:15]). For there is no other way of being a Christian. There is no way of making the kingdom present in the world except from within, impregnated with, transfigured by God, living in God and in God alone.

Paul wrote to the Galatians along the same lines: "But when the fullness of time had come, God sent his Son, born of a woman, born under the law, in order to redeem those who were under the law, so that we might receive adoption as children. And because you are children, God has sent the Spirit of his Son into our hearts, crying, 'Abba! Father!' So you are no longer a slave but a child, and if a child then also an heir, through God" (Gal 4:4–7). What wonders are hidden in the words of the *Our Father*. It contains the mystery of our sonship in Christ. We were made sons and daughters in the Son of God. Through Jesus, we entered into the very mystery of God, into the Heart of the Most Blessed Trinity. It is Christ who helps us to say "our Father." Left to ourselves, we were unable to pray, we would not have known to address God as our Father. We would not have known. This is what Jesus came to reveal to us. Every Christian is a consequence of Christ, and there is no Christian prayer that does not claim that its origin and key are fundamentally Christological. This is because Jesus the Good Shepherd carried us on his shoulders, ran to meet us, did not cease looking for us. It is because Jesus entered into the body of our ignorance and our fragility, that he revealed to us who we were. In our fragility we would not have had either the strength or the wisdom to say that God is our Father. It is precisely because Jesus took hold of us that we can pray to "our Father." And, for this reason, the *Our Father* is also the opposite of solitude. It is Jesus who enables us to discover at all times the mystery of God's love. If, at times, when we pray the *Our Father* our voice is weak, our soul wavering, and our petition a tremulous whisper, believing that he is with us gives us the strength we need.

WE ARE ONE

The words of Saint Cyprian on the *Our Father* are astonishingly clear:

> We do not say, "My Father, who art in heaven," nor "Give me this day my bread," nor does each one ask that only his [or her] debt be forgiven him [or her], and that he [or she] not be led into temptation and that he [or she] be delivered from evil for himself [or herself] alone. Our prayer is public and common, and when we pray, we pray not for one but for the whole people, because we, the whole people, are one.

Equally moving are the terms used by Saint Augustine: "'Our Father,' how great a condescension! This the emperor says, and this says the beggar: this says the slave and this his lord. They say all together….Therefore do they understand that they are brethren, seeing they have one Father."

The contemporary meditation of the poet Charles Péguy is along the same lines: "We must all be saved together, we all need to reach Paradise together; we must all arrive in Heaven together. We must think of others, we must give ourselves to others. What will God say to us if we appear in Heaven without the others?"

Before applying to each one of us, all these quotations, from Saint Cyprian to Péguy, apply perfectly to Jesus. He was precisely the One who did not wish to save himself on his own, but with the others. He wished to give himself; he did not seek to enter alone into his glory. When he entered into Paradise, he did so as the first-born Son, that is, as the head, as the first, the prototype. As we read in the Letter to the Romans: "He is the first-born among many brethren" (Rom 8:29). When we recite the *Our Father* we are being called to live an adventure that Jesus wanted to be like this: leave behind our human and common experience, our wounded living, in order to discover that he is accompanying us, as he accompanied the disciples on the way to Emmaus that afternoon which is now ours.

5

WHERE ARE YOU?
"…Who Art in Heaven"

It is important for us to remember, if only in order to understand fully what we have been saying, that God is not merely a model living inside us. He is not merely an internal *imago*, a presence in our interior life. God is an absolute presence in Himself. He does not merely exist within us as our point of reference, but exists ineffably in Himself. The scholastic theologians teach that while we ourselves are existences, God is essence. This is a definition that is perhaps easy to perceive with the intellect but extremely difficult to take in completely. If we are existences, we cannot easily conceive, beyond all existences, what essence alone might be. This difficulty tells us a great deal about the transcendental abyss that separates us from God and from this infinite that sets us apart. Simone Weil saw this in a positive light: "We must be happy in the knowledge that God is infinitely beyond our reach. Thus, we can be certain that the evil in us, even if it overwhelms our whole being, in no way sullies the divine purity, bliss, and perfection. We cannot take a single step toward him. We do not walk vertically. We can only turn our eyes toward him. We do not have to search for him, we only have to change the direction in which we are looking. It is for him to search for us." In fact, it is He who searches for us. We only seek God because God sought us first. It was He who stirred up in us the thirst we feel to see his face—our hunger for silence and for an encounter, our lack of the absolute, our longing for love, and for a love that never dies....

A GOD WHO IS

"Our Father, who art in heaven." Before commenting on the meaning of heaven, let us pause and reflect on the actual words. This is an astonishing statement which runs right through the biblical revelation, both the Old and New Testaments. God is. The transcendent God "sees," "listens," "has compassion," "appears," "makes the encounter possible." Think about the basic passage in the Book of Exodus:

> I have observed the misery of my people who are in Egypt; I have heard their cry on account of their taskmasters. Indeed, I know their sufferings, and I have come down to deliver them from the Egyptians, and to bring them up out of that land to a good and broad land, a land flowing with milk and honey....The cry of the Israelites has now come to me; I have also seen how the Egyptians oppress them. (Exod 3:7–9)

Scripture is sparing in definitions; instead it constructs a predominantly narrative grammar. It does not conceptualize: it narrates, describes, illustrates. The images that it offers us of God assure us that He is indeed close to us, aware of our hopes and the beating of our heart, always watching us, always nearby loving us: when all is said and done, a God who is. This is emphasized to such an extent that commentators on the Bible have asked themselves whether perhaps, in some places, the Bible has not gone too far, calling divine transcendence into question. A well-known example is the unforgettable Psalm 23 (22):

The Lord is my shepherd, I shall not want.
    He makes me lie down in green pastures;
he leads me beside still waters;
    he restores my soul.
He leads me in right paths
    for his name's sake.

Even though I walk through the darkest valley,
    I fear no evil;
for you are with me;
    your rod and your staff—
    they comfort me.

You prepare a table before me
    in the presence of my enemies;
you anoint my head with oil;
    my cup overflows.
Surely goodness and mercy shall follow me
    all the days of my life,
and I shall dwell in the house of the Lord
    my whole life long.

The crux of the problem is in verse 4: "Even though I walk through the darkest valley, I fear no evil; for you are with me." What is being said here? The "darkest valley" is the hellish places, the land of twilight, the descent into darkness, the decline into death. Does it make sense for the psalmist to declare: "You are with me"? Can God go down into dark places? Can He go down into the depths? Can He launch out on the nocturnal waters of those places of ours without hope? Can God go right down there, to what is unthinkable for God? Only the measurelessness of his love assures us that no shadow, no darkness is capable of obscuring the fidelity of his presence, and the assurance that He is with us in all the dramatic events in our lives.

Nothing restricts Him, nothing stops Him, nothing ties Him down. God is, ever and always.

With the same spiritual density of Psalm 23 (22), we need to reflect on this detail recorded by the evangelists in the account of Jesus' Passion: "And the Scripture was fulfilled which says: 'He was reckoned with the transgressors'" (Mark 15:28). The just man can be reckoned among sinners, and as if he were one of them? What is here spelled out is an astonishing mystery of solidarity and presence that leaves us speechless.

In one of his books, Elie Wiesel describes an execution in a concentration camp. A number of innocent people were called out at random and placed in the line of fire. One of those watching could not resist whispering: "O God, where are You?"—only to hear the whispered voice of a companion assuring him: "God is right there among those being shot."

THE ONTOLOGY OF THE DAILY ROUND

An Italian philosopher, Maurizio Ferraris, wrote a book that to some extent parodies our contemporary world, but that is disturbingly enlightening. The book is called *Where Are You? An Ontology of the Mobile Phone* (2006). Obviously, there cannot be an ontology of the mobile phone, but one can study the impact this and other technical innovations have had on life and behavior in today's world. When we made a call from a land line, we usually asked, "Are you there?" but presupposing that this was so if someone in fact answered the phone. With the proliferation of mobile phones, we have given up asking the rhetorical question "Are you there?" and the most usual question now is "Where are you?" We all seem to have become de-territorialized. We overvalue mobility to the detriment of permanence. We cease to "be" and to "know how to be." At best, we keep going without actually moving, fluctuating, sporadic, detached, vague.

An increasingly frequent experience is that of not having time. We say, repeating a saying from the days when Latin was a spoken language, that time flies (*tempus fugit*). The time for being flies. Nevertheless, "it was the time you wasted for your rose that makes your rose so important," explained the fox to the little Prince. Yes indeed, we know there is a quality of relationship that can only come with time. For some reason, that unusual Master of humanity called Jesus said: "If any one forces you to go one mile, go with him two miles." Only by remaining still can we discover the meaning and the point of our walking alongside others. Only by remaining present to ourselves can we take possession of our interior journey. It is so easy to become unknown entities. All we have to do is not to remain still.

Blaise Pascal used to say that human unhappiness comes from one thing only: not knowing how to remain still in one place. We seem to need to live seven lives in a single day, breathless, anxious, torn in different directions and suffering from insomnia. Somehow, we cannot manage our time peacefully. From prolonged work times to the almost unceasing calls on our attention, we are plunged into a breathless cycle of attention, activity, and consumption. "Hurry up, hurry up," urges a voice that holds us prisoner, uttered by someone we cannot see. "Go here, go there." Where are we going? It may well be that if we were asked to explain the deep reasons for our dizzy activity, for our rushing all over the place, for our constant moving from one thing to another, we would not be able to. And from this too, from this inability to reply, we prefer to flee.

Our God simply is! One possible way of translating the divine name *Yahweh* is the phrase "I am for you"; "I am for you." The author of the Letter to the Hebrews uses it in a lovely paraphrase: "God has said, 'I will never leave you or forsake you'" (Heb 13:5). It is a true declaration of love. The Risen Lord confirms and broadens its meaning, in the final discourse in the

Gospel of Saint Matthew: "I am with you always, to the end of the age" (Matt 28:20). Our God simply is!

A spiritually disastrous idea has entered into the current vision of Christian existence according to which, when we sin, God withdraws from us; that what happens is something like an eclipse of God. As if that could happen! On the contrary, we need to make it clear that when we sin, God clings to our necks. God does not leave us; God increases his love for us. God pours out his tenderness, He beckons to us, He begs us to wake up, to return to ourselves and remember who and what we are, to recover our strength....And it is exactly because God clings to our neck, like someone who loves us absolutely, someone who— as it says in the parable—"covers us with kisses" (Luke 15:20), that we can return to our Father's embrace. To plunge into the *Our Father* is to discover this God who is. And also to learn ourselves how to be.

GOD IS GREATER THAN THE HEAVENS

We pray, "Our Father, who art in heaven," and this is an invocation that we need to understand. Origen gives us this explanation: "When the Father of Saints is said to be in the heavens, we are not to suppose that He is circumscribed by material form and dwells in heaven. If this were the case, God would be less than the heavens because they contain Him, whereas the ineffable might of His godhead demands our belief that all things are contained and held together by Him." The heavens are God Himself, his being, his unspeakable glory. Symbolically, the heavens are above us; they are what covers us. They represent, essentially, the roof, the festive dance, the eschatological horizon of our very existence. We know that above everything there are the heavens. We know that the heavens do not cover us only on days of rejoicing, but also in times of sadness and suffering, the times when we come to a parting of the ways, when hope seems to have diminished. We know that no one place contains more heaven than another. A shrine does not contain more heaven than the place where we work, where we are involved in activity and in toil, practicing our profession, being of service to others....There is not more heaven above a welcoming roof than above the lonely road that we are travelling.

And the heavens have no frontiers. After all, we do not have to learn to speak another language, nor do we have to do anything special, because heaven is over us all the time. And for this reason, in its transversality this image is something that really does introduce into our heart this mystery of the presence of God.

To say "Our Father who art in heaven" is to say "Our Father" who is always, really and truly always....Who is everywhere, who keeps everything in your heart. "Our Father" here present, as He is present to my brother and sister. "Our Father," who comes from the very beginning and is at the same time the One who remains. Here on earth everything dies and is born, coming to life again and dying again, whereas the heavens are there always.

The Christian mystics bear witness to this, saying: "Stop, where are you running to?—Heaven is within you; if you are looking for God somewhere else you will never find Him."

Or, quite simply: "Stop, where are you running to? Heaven is within you...."

Lord, at times our prayer is no more than the touch of your hand, the absolute need to feel your wide-open hand, ready to welcome us just as we are into your silence; it is no more than the longing to feel the touch, be it ever so light, of your immensity in the rush, the precariousness, the uncertainty of our daily lives; it is no more than this need to recognize that, by simply being, You receive this kind of hunger and longing that we are.

6

TO GIVE A NAME WITHOUT LOSING WHAT CANNOT BE SAID

"Hallowed Be Your Name"

It is good for us believers to listen to what unbelievers have to say about God and the spiritual life. Speaking for myself, I can say that they teach us many things! The problem is that we run the risk of making things too easy, taking things for granted, reproducing things uncritically. I have a friend who says he is an atheist, and every time we meet he asks me: "Have you thought about God?" And when I ask him the same question, he replies: "I'd have you know that I think about nothing else." One of the symptoms of our having gone soft interiorly is our tendency to use stock answers, the self-justification of those who go in for short cuts, avoiding the exigencies and the delays involved in going the whole way. "My son, if you come forward to serve the Lord, prepare yourself for trials" (Sir 2:1). It is in trials and the tested dedication that intimacy calls for that the authentic spiritual life is to be found.

One day, a young writer came to the Rato Chapel, of which I am chaplain. As he was leaving, he said to me, "You ought to have the courage to remove all these chairs from this chapel where Christians are sitting much too comfortably, and spread on this floor, which is highly polished and stable, a good coating of earth, to remind us that faith presupposes much searching and unceasing journeys."

While thinking about the "Hallowed be thy name" petition in the *Our Father*, I was reminded of an admittedly austere poem by Eugenio de Andrade which, however, brings us back to the need to search. There are times when we need to begin again from the beginning, to feel that the summons to undertake a journey is more important than the chairs. Or, as Don Quixote used to say, that the road has more to teach us than the hostelry.

Eugenio de Andrade's poem is called "O Inominável" (The Nameless One):

> Never
> did you place your ear
> close to my lips; never
> did you bring your lips close to my ear;
> you are silence,
> the hard thick impenetrable
> silence without images.
> We listen to, drink the silence
> in our own hands
> and nothing unites us
> —we do not even know if you have a name.

IT MUST ALWAYS BE DIFFICULT TO SPEAK ABOUT GOD, AND THIS IS A GOOD THING

In the first epistle of Saint John, we read that "God abides in us and his love is perfected in us," but also that "No one has ever seen God" (1 John 4:12). The Catholic poet Charles Péguy prays as follows in one of his odes:

You remind me of the great silence
that there was in the world
before the kingdom of men was established.
You foretell for me the great silence there will be in the
    world
when the kingdom of men comes to an end.

It is true that we do not know whether God has a name. It is also true that both believers and unbelievers drink God's silence in their own hands. God cannot be manipulated or tamed by means of speeches and representations. The biblical revelation, for example, is very careful to preserve the "unsayability" of God. "Why is it that you ask my name?" was God's reply to the Patriarch Jacob's question while they were still locked in combat (Gen 32:30). In the culture of the biblical world, to know someone's name was to have power over, or some kind of equality with, that particular person. And this is still true today. We have more power, however fictitious, over someone whose name we know than over someone that we see in the street and whose name we do not know nor where he or she is going. By broadening out this way of thinking, the Bible will also deprive us of the ability to see the face of God. God is there beyond what we are capable of perceiving. God is always beyond us, God is always Other in relation to what we are capable of knowing.

The experience of faith should lead us to recognize that God is God and that this involves a literal plunging into a radically different reality. The experience is built up in the intransigent, disconcerting, and glowing oxymoron that is its primary figure; faith is the thirst that slakes one's thirst, the hunger that satisfies one's hunger, the vacuum that is filled with plenitude, the darkness filled with shining light. It is in our praying poverty, with our hands stretched out and empty, that we can touch it and live.

There is undoubtedly room for a positive theological formulation. We can in fact say some valid things about God. But

this intelligible knowledge has been defined in the patristic tradition as "symbolic" and "merely symbolic," since the transcendent reality cannot be reduced to any system of thought.
Gregory of Nyssa warns that "concepts create idols" when we use
them in order to proclaim God. In his view, "the mystery is
revealed beyond any knowledge, beyond any ignorance, in the
most luminous darkness of silence, that darkness which can be
perceived only by prayerful contemplation." It is an approximation such as this that faith gives us.

As method, it does not deal in speculation. Faith does not
communicate knowledge, does not provide routes, does not repeat
itself. "Go where you cannot go / see where you cannot see / listen
where there is no sound and so you will be where God speaks,"
whispers the mystic Angelus Silesius. The only route is that of a
progressive stripping off, of trusting abandonment and transformation. True prayer is the prayer one prays without images: it is
to expose oneself, stripped naked or, as the Song of Songs puts it,
it is the nuptial encounter. The person praying is called to remain
hidden within his or her own manifestation. "You have died and
your life is hidden with Christ in God" (Col 3:3).

In what is, perhaps, one of the most ardent autobiographies
of the soul written in the twentieth century, that of Mother Teresa
of Calcutta, we find, to the dismay and shock of those whose
acquaintance with Christianity is merely sociological, the
essence of Christian mysticism. How not to love the harshness,
the purification, the defenseless essentiality, the being laid open,
the acknowledged misery of this astonishing woman who prayed
like this: "Don't mind my feelings," and who said of God "I want
to love God for what He takes. There is so much contradiction
in my soul. Such deep longing for God—so deep that it is
painful—a suffering continual—and yet not wanted by God—
repulsed—empty—no faith—no love—no zeal. Souls hold no
attraction—Heaven means nothing—to me it looks like an

empty place—the thought of it means nothing to me and yet this torturing longing for God...." And she ended up by saying: "If I ever become a Saint—I will surely be one of 'darkness.'"

BLESSED DARKNESS

This is what needs to be said because the great risk for our spiritual journey is rarely the "dark night," rarely doubts about our faith, the aridity of the desert, times of turbulence, struggles....The great danger is for there not to be any waves, for everything to be excessively normal, linear, utilitarian, functional. We can revolt a thousand times against the so-called "philosophers of suspicion," and we do not see that, long before them and perhaps much more seriously than in their case, we believers have excluded God, the living God, from our own lives. We make Him into a reference from the past, a history we already know, a guidebook we have already read, carefully preserved in the fold of the present, a kind of private archaeology for a monotonous purpose.

One of the most striking books about religious anxiety is undoubtedly *The Brothers Karamazov*. The best-known part of the book is the section known as "The Legend of the Grand Inquisitor" and relates a story that cannot fail to make us think. It is set at the time of the Inquisition in Spain, in the city of Seville. "In his infinite mercy, Jesus walked once again among men, in the same human image in which he had walked for three years among men during his public life on earth....He appeared quietly, inconspicuously but—strange to say—everyone recognized him. People were drawn to him by an invincible force, they flocked to him, surrounded him, followed him. He passed silently among them with a quiet smile of infinite compassion. The sun of love shone in his heart, rays of Light, Enlightenment, and Power streamed from his eyes and, pouring over the people, shook their hearts with responding love. He stretched forth his hands to them, blessed them, and from the touch of him, even only of his garments, came a healing power. Here an old man, blind from childhood, called out from the crowd, *'Lord, heal me so that I, too, can see you,'* and it was as if the scales fell from his eyes, and the blind man saw him. People were weeping with joy and kissing the earth he walked on. Children threw down flowers before him, singing and calling out: *'Hosanna! It **is** he, it really is he*; everyone repeated, *'It must be he.'* He stopped at the porch of the Seville cathedral at the very moment when a child's little, open white coffin was being brought in with weeping; in it lay a seven-year-old girl, the only daughter of a noble citizen. The dead child was covered with flowers. *'He will raise your child,'* people in the crowd shouted to the weeping mother. The cathedral padre, who had come out to meet the coffin, looked perplexed and frowned. Suddenly a wail came from the dead child's mother. She threw herself down at his feet: *'If it is you, then raise my child,'* she exclaimed, stretching her hands out to him. The procession halted, the little coffin was lowered down onto the porch at his feet. He looked with compassion and his lips once again softly uttered: *'Talitha cumi'*—and the damsel arose."

At this very moment, the Cardinal Grand Inquisitor appeared at the end of the street and, seeing what had happened and recognizing that it was in fact Jesus, ordered his arrest. That night, he went in secret to have a talk with him. For a Christian conscience, there is no dialogue that is more disturbing. Summing it all up, the Grand Inquisitor said to Jesus: "You can no longer do anything; what you had to do has been done; what you had to say has been said....Now it is we who keep going/maintain what you said. You cannot come again with miracles, you cannot come raising people from the dead again. Now things are in order and you too are boxed in within this order."

Very often, this is what our religiosity amounts to. We say:

God is this, his name is that. And God has to remain there boxed in, tamed. And we spend most of our lives saying to God: "You can't"; "You can't." This is a fundamental aspect of our conversion. To discover, deep within myself, whether or not I make space for God to continue to say things, for God to continue to be, for God to go where He wishes to go and not merely where I think He ought to go.

In the much commented-on speech that he made in the Auschwitz-Birkenau Concentration Camp in May of 2006, Pope Benedict XVI said: "We cannot peer into God's mysterious plan—we see only piecemeal, and we would be wrong to set ourselves up as judges….The God in whom we believe is a God of reason—a reason, to be sure, which is not a kind of cold mathematics. […] In a place like this, words fail; in the end, there can only be a dread silence—a silence which is itself a heartfelt cry to God."

In order to respect the presence of God, I, too, seek to remain living before God. Because this is the other side of the medallion….If you will pardon the crudeness of the expression, if I treat God like someone who is fixed in an image or an undefined concept, I, too, release myself from the need to be living before Him. And then, we go on our way before God, bodily present but without really being involved. We do not really go in, we do not commit ourselves….

What we need, perhaps, are new words in our prayer. We need them, in fact, in order to give meaning to the extraordinary prayers that we have inherited from the treasury of tradition. We need to articulate once again the experience of God in our everyday language. To say, in our own words, that God is the way, God is the gateway, God is the ship, God is the shining thread, God is the running water, God is the face of a child, God is the unbroken shaft of light, God is the day who drives away the night…. Using either traditional words or the language of today, we must become capable of maintaining a living relationship with God, and of feeling ourselves alive before Him. Our relationship with God is a living relationship.

THERE IS BUT ONE SADNESS, NOT TO BE SAINTS

In that well-known story "O retrato de Mónica" [The Portrait of Monica], Sophia de Mello Breyner Andresen explains that poetry is given to us once only and when we refuse it, it is withdrawn. Love is given to us several times, and in the same way if we reject it, it leaves us. But the possibility of holiness is given to us every day. And if we refuse it, we shall have to reject it all the days of our life, because holiness approaches us every day as a possibility.

However, we have turned holiness into something so extraordinary, abstract, and unattainable that we are almost afraid to speak about it. In a way, we grow accustomed to regarding Christian experience as something that happens on two levels: the heroic path of the saints and the fragile path followed by everyone else, ourselves most of all. Now, this concept of holiness could not be further from the one presented to us by Christian tradition. The Second Vatican Council, for example, makes this very clear: holiness is the most common and inclusive vocation (*Lumen Gentium*, ch. V). But we need to understand what we are talking about when we are talking about holiness.

It would be enough for us to read the Beatitudes. Jesus did not say that the Beatitudes were for others, the people who were not there. Jesus looked round at the crowd and began to say: "Blessed are you poor," "Blessed are you who mourn," "Blessed are you who show mercy." What does this mean? That it is our own poverty, fragility, pains and aches, meekness, longings, and thirst that give substance to the beatitude, that are the material of holiness. It is what we are and do, in the very ordinary map of all we seek, in the humble and even monotonous geography that locates us, in the trivial day-to-day story in which we play a part every day that we can link earth to heaven. To speak of holiness in a Christian key comes down to this: to believe that the humanity of human beings has become the dwelling place of the divine, of God.

A story is told about a housewife who also wished to found a sect, as she did not want to fall behind others and look on at the daily spectacle of the proliferation of such sects. So she decided to found one herself in which she herself and her housemaid would be, so to speak, the "gurus" and prophets of this new piece of madness. And in it she began, in fact, to acquire a certain importance, and it was always herself and her housemaid, her housemaid and herself....After some time, some journalists came to interview her. Naturally, they wished to speak to the lady of the house and they asked her:

"Are you happy?"
"Very, I am very pleased with the church that I founded,
    but now I am thinking of founding another!"
"You are already thinking about another one?"
"Yes, I think there ought to be a sect in which I alone am
    the prophet."

To say "Hallowed be thy name" is to avoid living in accordance with those experiences of God which are manifestly egotistical and inadequate. It is to be brave, to dare to say: "God be God in me. Teach me to be a disciple, faithful in listening to, being receptive to, the promptings of the Spirit, to the apprenticeship of the Word, ready to comply with its historical implications. Thy name, O God, is a 'non-name'; it challenges me to be ready, day by day, to listen to your name. Let me not lock myself inside a comfortable storeroom of certainties, but rather to look with fresh eyes at the paths, whether expected or unexpected that You point to for me...."

Over the entrance to a twelfth-century monastery in Toledo, there is a notice that says: "There are no paths, one must just walk." To say "Hallowed be thy name" is thus to commit ourselves to being pilgrims in the name of God; it is to take upon oneself Abraham's situation, the situation of the entire People of God who became pilgrims in the name and the face of God, the situation of Jesus who "had nowhere to lay his head," creating a history of holiness and nothing more.

"Be holy, for I, your God, am holy" (Lev 11:45). The writer Léon Bloy used to say: "There is but one sadness, not to be saints." And yet, as Sophia de Mello Breyner Andresen makes clear, holiness is given to us as a real possibility every day: "Holiness is offered anew to each one of us every day, so much so that those who say 'no' to holiness are obliged to repeat their refusal every day." It is as a challenge to a living holiness that Saint Cyprian, too, explains this segment of the *Our Father*. He urged: "Let us petition and ask for this, that we who have been sanctified in baptism may persevere in what we have begun. And for this daily do we pray. For we have need of daily sanctification, that we who sin daily may cleanse our sins by continual sanctification."

The flower of the world is holiness. This form of God present at all times, in all latitudes, in all cultures. What saves the world is holiness: it gives flexibility to hardness, reunites what is divided, gives freedom to prisoners, instills hope in the hearts of the downhearted, conceals bread in the lap of those who are hungry, embraces the pain of those who mourn, and dances with those who experience joy. Holiness is a hidden furrow, but sheds light all round it. Holiness is anonymous and unostentatious. It is not heroic: it expresses itself in what is small, in the everyday, in what is ordinary. Sin is the banality of evil. Holiness is the normality of goodness. As we see in this poem by Maria de Lourdes Belchior:

Today is the day of All Saints: of those who have a halo
and of those who were not canonised.
The day of All Saints: of those who lived serenely
and quietly without attracting attention and who,
    at the end
of time, will be following the Lamb.
Today is the day of all saints, saints who were barbers,
saints who were cooks, played football and, why not?
businessmen, merchants, boiler makers
and ushers (including female ushers, since it is
frequently they who show people to their seats?)
Down through the centuries, in the silence of the night and
in broad daylight they were all your witnesses;
they said yes/yes and no/no; they wasted
few words in circumlocutions, digressions. They were
your imitators and in the transparency of their gestures
your image was clearly visible. Adventurers and others,
whether daring or timid and docile,
they carried you in their hearts,
they looked lovingly at the world and
at men and women as their brothers and sisters.
From the ground they trod
arose the hope of a future
of justice and salvation,
and the present, for them, was almost only love.
A countless cortège of men and women who
followed you and lived with you, admirably:
they shared their bread with those who were hungry,
they looked with compassion on the sufferings
of the world and endured persecution for the sake
    of justice.
They were pure of heart and so
purity shone in their eyes and from their lips

issued words of consolation.
They loved you and they loved the world.
They sang your praise and the beauty of Creation.
And they wept for the pains of those in despair.
They could make gestures of indignation and utter
prophetic words which could rend clear horizons.
They are those who follow the Lamb
because they knew you and recognised you
and from you they received
the gift of proclaiming justice and salvation to the world.

To say "Hallowed be thy name" is to say to God: Be whole, do not let me divide You or diminish You through my egoism and my moods....Be as You are, show Yourself in me and in all, reveal Yourself in all that is different from me or opposed to me, in all that goes against me. Do not let me be a brake on your love. May your holiness, O God, be a star that leads us, the column of fire that goes ahead of us, the shepherd's whistle that is our signal....In our humility, we are the tent in which God sets up camp in this world of ours, and every day we move forward, in a different place, a new way....As Saint Augustine wrote: "The holiness of God's Name is our holiness." Believers are not the managers of an outward action: they are servants and travelers, nomads and enamored pilgrims, readers and listeners, dedicated adorers....

7

LEARNING TO LIVE ACCORDING TO GOD'S WILL
"Thy Kingdom Come"

Saint Augustine says something that is both curious and certain about the petition "Thy kingdom come." "When we say, 'Thy kingdom come,' which shall certainly come whether we wish it or not, we do by these words stir up our own desires for that kingdom." It is true. Essentially, Christianity is an initiation into desire. A school of desire. Simone Weil's commentary on these words points in the same direction: "The Kingdom of God means the complete filling of the entire soul...with the Holy Spirit. The Spirit bloweth where he listeth. We can only invite him. [...] We must just invite him purely and simply, so that our thought is an invitation, a longing cry."

At times I am assailed by the fear that we are constructing an excessively crystallized Christianity with everything put in its proper place, a perfect organigram, a well-oiled machine, but with no horizon, as if we were (I apologize for the analogy) a "maps and tourist guide department" and not an association of explorers, mountain climbers, sailors, and travelers.

I often think of what Françoise Dolto says in the introduction to her psychoanalytic reading of the Gospels. For years, she declares, she had listened to the sacred texts merely as if they were historic or moral documents. And the truth is that they

55

barely skimmed above life in its concrete reality. The turning point came when she realized that the Scriptures are "a school of desire" since they inscribe deep within us "an effect of truth" capable of initiating us into freedom and love.

It is not, in fact, the stored-up knowledge of a day that can serve us as a map, but our reflection on what has happened. We are being called to go on a pilgrimage, to assess the depth in movement, to glimpse, in and through all we see on our way, that which is permanent. Our eyes do not always recognize that they are poor, but when they do, then at last they perceive the truth contained in a line of poetry by Rainer Maria Rilke and in many other places: "Poverty is a great glow from within." Then there are the wise words of the mystic Saint John of the Cross:

> To reach satisfaction in all
>   desire satisfaction in nothing.
> To come to the knowledge of all
>   desire the knowledge of nothing.
> To come to possess all
>   desire the possession of nothing.
> To arrive at being all
>   desire to be nothing.
> To come to enjoy what you have not
>   you must go by a way in which you enjoy not.
> To come to the knowledge you have not
>   you must go by a way in which you know not.
> To come to the possession you have not
>   you must go by a way in which you possess not.
> To come to be what you are not
>   you must go by a way in which you are not.

GO BEYOND THE BOOK

Christianity makes a fundamental shift in the religious universe. It ceases to be a "religion of the Book" in order to become the "religion of Someone." It is a religion that is born of a Person and is centered on that Person. Saint Luke states this very clearly, as if we were watching a film: "Jesus came to Nazareth, where he had been brought up; and he went to the synagogue, as his custom was, on the Sabbath day. And he stood up to read; and there was given to him the book of the prophet Isaiah. He opened the book and found the place where it was written, 'The Spirit of the Lord is upon me, because he has anointed me to preach good news to the poor. He has sent me to proclaim release to the captives and recovering of sight to the blind, to set at liberty those who are oppressed, to proclaim the acceptable year of the Lord.' He then closed the book, gave it back to the attendant and sat down; and the eyes of all in the synagogue were fixed on him. And he began to say to them, 'Today this scripture has been fulfilled in your hearing'" (Luke 4:16–21).

Jesus takes the book and reads one of the passages concerning the mission of the Messiah as foretold by the prophet Isaiah. This text was in the hearts of all; it had been passed on from generation to generation, complete with a note of interrogative hope: "When will the one who brings good news to the poor, who heals the broken-hearted, gives sight to the blind, releases the captives, proclaims an acceptable year of the Lord, a year of the marvels of the Lord, be coming?"

Jesus reads the text, closes the book, and returns it to the attendant. At that moment, symbolically but also in a very real way, Jesus goes beyond the book and sits down. When Jesus speaks while seated, what he says becomes particularly solemn. So Jesus sits down. He is there as a Teacher, with all the authority of the Messiah. And he says: "Today this scripture has been fulfilled in your hearing." He begins to speak to them. He has moved on from "the Book to the Person." A new threshold has been reached with Jesus of Nazareth. The time of the prophets has ended, for we have among us the one who is the subject of the prophecies, the Messiah. An end has come to the time when God's action was merely foretold at some future date ("when the Messiah comes, when his time has come") because in Jesus the "today," the "now" of God's salvation has come. There is no longer any need to live on prophecies, because the One who was foretold has arrived. There is now no need for hope, since the One who was hoped for has come. The mystery of the Incarnation enables us to believe that God's mercy, in the history of mankind, has ceased to be sealed in the letters of a book, and has become a life, an existence, a living reality. A here-and-now, where God becomes present. It is not by chance that Jesus' first proclamation was "The kingdom of God is at hand," or "The kingdom of God is within you."

WHAT IS THE KINGDOM OF GOD?

The kingdom of God is not described conceptually, but in a narrative key. What we can say is that it is inseparable from Jesus, from this *now* of God's salvation, this *outpouring* of his grace in history. It is inseparable from this *tearing apart* of history in favor of the poor and the unhappy, this *balm* poured out on broken hearts, this *word* of encouragement for those who had given up hoping; from this *drawing* concrete lives *close to* the possibility of God's salvation. Wherever Jesus went, the kingdom went too. Wherever Jesus was, the kingdom of God appeared. When people touched Jesus, they were touching the kingdom; when they saw him, they were seeing the kingdom. When they were listening to his parables, they were listening to the hidden grammar of the kingdom. Jesus lived his life as an extraordinary manifestation of the kingdom. The kingdom of God coincided with the presence of Jesus, and what extraordinary effects this produced in many lives. People who felt they were dead, who were thought to be lost, in a hopelessly entangled existence from which there seemed no escape…in Jesus Christ discovered the possibility of a new life. Think, for instance, of Mary Magdalene, the one whom Jesus had released from seven devils. We have no idea what it can be like to be possessed by seven devils….We can imagine to ourselves what it must be like for such a person, in terms of total breakdown, going to pieces, inability to pull oneself together. The truth is that this woman, rejected and alienated from herself, finds herself in Jesus Christ and in him rediscovers a desire to be. Think, too, of the lives of the disciples, who certainly already knew a great many things about God but who, in Jesus Christ, heard things that they did not know. They already knew how to sail on the sea of Galilee, but they did not know how to walk on the waves; they already knew how to gather up and distribute bread, but they did not know how to multiply it, they did not know that bread can also satisfy an inner hunger, the hunger of the heart.

Think of sinners, those who were pointed at scornfully and about whom it was said: "They are beyond salvation." How surprised Zacchaeus must have been as he came down from the tree in order to welcome Jesus into his house. Or Levi, who got up and left his tax office in order to become a disciple….This is the kingdom of God here and now. This is the kingdom of God at work: a kingdom without frontiers, not according to human logic, but in an ever-increasing flood of divine love, like an incoming tide that seeks to touch everything and everyone.

"The kingdom of God is in the midst of you." We are not to say that it is here or there. The kingdom of God is present as a reality in itself. The kingdom of God belongs to God and not to our temptation to impose limits, to erect barriers, to separate. "Being asked by the Pharisees when the kingdom of God was coming, he answered them, 'The kingdom of God is not coming with signs to be observed; nor will they say, "Lo, here it is!" or "There!" for behold, the kingdom of God is in the midst of you'" (Luke 17:20–21).

This is Jesus' great announcement: "The kingdom of God is in the midst of you!" It is within you, in the middle of the world, within history as a seed….This is the wonderful treasure waiting to be discovered. God is already here! And what we need is to become aware of this presence. The kingdom of God is already a reality, is already a ferment….And although it is true that the kingdom of God also represents an eschatological reality, a reality of the future, something which has yet to come in its fullness, the truth is that, although we realize that it is a future gift, the kingdom of God is already a reality of today in my life. Today my life is enfolded in the kingdom of God. "The kingdom of God is as if a man should scatter seed upon the ground, and should sleep and rise night and day, and the seed should sprout and grow, he knows not how" (Mark 4:26–27).

The medieval alchemists used to say: "Without a drop of gold, it is impossible to make gold." Similarly, without a drop of the kingdom of God, we cannot construct the kingdom of God, we cannot pray for it, we cannot even hope for it. When all is said and done, the kingdom of God summarizes all hope. It is that reality of God that mysteriously meshes gears with the most intimate of hopes. Because, in God's kingdom, we have fullness, we have the concretization of the love of God. All we need is the kingdom of God; everything else will be added. And relative….

THY KINGDOM COME

"The law and the prophets were until John; since then the good news of the kingdom of God is preached, and every one enters it violently" (Luke 16:16). The kingdom is a gift ("Fear not, little flock, for it is your Father's good pleasure to give you the kingdom" [Luke 12:32]), but it is also a toil, an effort that calls for a peaceful but energetic violence. This violence is certainly not that of the sword, nor of discord, which is the seed of the devil. The violence of which Jesus speaks means that the kingdom of God must be in us a power. We need energy in order to build up the kingdom of God step by step. The kingdom of God does not come about through being passive.

We must pray: "Thy kingdom come, Lord! Let your kingdom prevail over all our winters, all our sterilities, our deserts, our failures and weakness, let your kingdom be a burgeoning spring. A resurgence of life." Our commitment to the kingdom in fact pledges our energy, our creativity, our very breath....We need this gentle turbulence every day of our lives. If we are not engaged in constructing the kingdom of God, we are busy constructing one of our own. We need to say a "yes" that is a real yes, and a "no" that is a real no. The kingdom of God needs this energy. It is not something that comes ready-made, it is in the process of being built, of becoming.

The kingdom of God requires our entire lives, all our moments, all our strength. The kingdom of God exacts from us our energy, our sweat. It does not ask us for things, but for ourselves. The kingdom of God requires us to be there present. But at the same time we must not forget that the kingdom of God is not ours. The kingdom of God pledges us and goes beyond us. We are the keepers of the kingdom not its owners. We are the ones who proclaim the kingdom, not its proprietors.

"Thy kingdom come." Jesus has already come, he has lived, he has already revealed himself, he has already become intimate with all human beings. But today he continues to come, he continues to make himself present, he continues to speak to the hearts of men and women through his Church, which is animated by the Spirit of the Risen One. The Church is the Sacrament of

Christ. The Church is one with the mystery of the Incarnation, which is not yet complete. Pascal used to say: "The mystery of the Passion of Christ continues until the end of time." But we can also say that the Mystery of the Lord's Incarnation continues to take place until end of time. Jesus' mission continues to be written in and through ourselves.

To ask for the kingdom of God to come is to ask that the name which we bear, the name of a Christian man or woman, in fact, possesses the vitality of Christ within it. It also means that we feel that we are sharing in the ministry of Christ. We have been anointed in order to make this kingdom present in this world, a kingdom of justice and peace, a kingdom of joy and hope, a kingdom of forgiveness and love, a kingdom of rejoicing, a kingdom of reconciliation.

There is a poem by Sophia de Mello Breyner Andresen that can be read as a prayer:

> I call you because everything is still only beginning
> And to endure is the longest time.
>
> I ask you to come and give me freedom,
> For just one glance from you to purify me, and that's that.
>
> There are many things that I do not want to see.
>
> I ask you to be the present.
> I ask you to fill everything.
> And for your kingdom to come sooner than expected
> And be poured out on the Earth
> Bursting forth like spring on the earth.

8

WE STILL HAVE A CHILDHOOD TO LIVE

"Thy Will Be Done on Earth as It Is in Heaven"

The first time the expression "Let there be" appears in the Bible is on the very first page (Gen 1:3–31). And these words are spoken by God Himself. He continues, "Let there be light," and there was light. And God saw that the light was good. And God said, "Let there be an evening and a morning" and there was the first day. God said, "Let there be light in the firmament of the heavens." And it was so. And so on.

Behind each created thing there is God's "Let there be," his "Yes." There is nothing, from the grass in the field to the lonely mountain, from the powerful animal to the rag of a cloud, from the first light of dawn to the dusk of evening, that is not the astonishing result of a "Yes" spoken by the Creator. Behind each creature, we can hear the music of God's loving summons. Francis of Assisi was right in perceiving a universal brotherhood, calling the water, the sun, the rain, and the fire his brothers and sisters. If we really think about it, life and creation can only be contemplated on our knees. Everywhere we look, we perceive the astonishing coming of God. Most certain are the words that the poet Walt Whitman sings: "I believe a leaf of grass is no less than the journey work of the stars.... / And the tree-toad is a chef-d'oeuvre for the highest.... / And a mouse is miracle enough to stagger sextillions of infidels."

Antoine Saint-Exupéry explained: "What makes the desert beautiful…is that somewhere it hides a well…." What makes ourselves beautiful and lights up beauty all round us? This secret that is hidden in life: the pulse of God, his endless throbbing. When we perceive this, we find that we at last believe that Creation is God's great cathedral! It is God's great Tabernacle, a natural shrine where God is really and truly present. Everything is "Let there be"; everything is a manifestation of his will.

It is this that Pierre Teilhard de Chardin left written in his magnificent spiritual testament that is his *Mass on the World*:

> Since once again, Lord—though this time not in the forests of the Aisne but in the steppes of Asia—I have neither bread, nor wine, nor altar, I will raise myself beyond these symbols, up to the pure majesty of the Real itself. I, your priest, will make the whole earth my altar and on it will offer you all the labors and sufferings of the world. Over there, on the horizon, the sun has just touched with light the outermost fringe of the eastern sky. Once again, beneath this moving sheet of fire, the living surface of the earth wakes and trembles, and once again begins its fearful travail. I will place on my paten, O God, the harvest to be won by this renewal of labor. Into my chalice I shall pour all the sap which is to be pressed out this day from the earth's fruits. My paten and my chalice are the depths of a soul laid widely open to all the forces which in a moment will rise up from every corner of the earth and converge upon the Spirit. Grant me the remembrance and the mystic presence of all those whom the light is now awakening to the new day!

[…] Once upon a time men took into your temple the first fruits of their harvests, the flower of their flocks. But the offering you really want, the offering you mysteriously need every day to appease your hunger, to slake your thirst is nothing less than the growth of the world borne ever onwards in the stream of universal becoming. Receive, O Lord, this all-embracing host which your whole creation, moved by your magnetism, offers you at this dawn of a new day. This bread, our toil, is of itself, I know, but an immense fragmentation; this wine, our pain, is no more, I know, than a draught that dissolves. Yet in the very depths of this formless mass you have implanted —and this I am sure of, for I sense it—a desire, irresistible, hallowing, which makes us cry out, believer and unbeliever alike: "Lord, make us One!"

THE ENDLESS DANCE OF CREATION

The language of the Genesis poem becomes suddenly more solemn when it begins to speak of human beings. Instead of "Let there be," God said, "Let us make…," making use of a mysterious plural. "Let us make man in our image, after our likeness…" (Gen 1:26). And that is where we come from, in a way that we do not know. It will be for science to explain it, although it will be difficult to do away with the enigma. What is important, for the wisdom of Faith, is that, in whatever form we first appeared on earth, in the beginning there was the "Let there be" of God. We exist thanks to this "Yes."

The Incarnation of Jesus Christ was the second Creation, as we are told by the Fathers of the Church, an authentic recreation of the landscape of the world and of human beings. The world is no longer merely the original cosmos, but a redeemed world.

We are not merely the offspring of Adam. "'Behold, I make all things new,' said the One who sat upon the throne" (Rev 21:5). "In Christ Jesus you are all children of God, through faith. For as many of you as were baptized into Christ have put on Christ. There is neither Jew nor Greek, there is neither slave nor free, there is neither male nor female; for you are all one in Christ Jesus" (Gal 3:6–28). The mystery of this second Creation of the world also depends on a number of "Let there be" commands. We have Mary's *Fiat!* Mary, who said: "Behold the handmaid of the Lord, be it done unto me according to your word" (Luke 1:38). Mary's readiness to be available made possible the mystery of the Incarnation and united her inseparably, like a seamless garment, to the saving Mystery of her own Son. The life of Mary can be read in two parts: before this word and after it. The key to her life was this "Let it be done to me according to thy will."

And then, of course, we have, the ongoing "Let there be" of Jesus himself. He admitted to his disciples: "My food is to do the will of him who sent me, and to accomplish his work" (John 4:34). At the very moment when he was about to complete his work, at the doorway to the Passion, he fell on his face and prayed: "'My Father, if it be possible, let this cup pass from me; nevertheless, not as I will, but as thou wilt.'…Again, for the second time, he went away and prayed, 'My Father, if this cannot pass unless I drink it, thy will be done'" (Matt 26, 39, 42). In the magnificent meditation on this passage that we find in the Letter to the Hebrews, we read: "When Christ came into the world, he said: 'Sacrifices and offerings thou hast not desired, but a body hast thou prepared for me; in burnt offerings and sin offerings thou hast taken no pleasure.' Then I said: 'Lo, I have come to do thy will, O God,' as it is written of me in the roll of the book" (Heb 10:5–7).

But the dance of creation continues. Every day, when we pray the *Our Father*, we too have an opportunity to say our own *fiat*. Indeed, we absolutely need this opportunity. Once again, the author of the Letter to the Hebrews gives us the words we need: "You have need of endurance, so that you may do the will of God and receive what is promised. For yet a little while, and the coming one shall come and shall not tarry" (Heb 10:36–37). Might it be possible to divide our own lives, too, into two parts: before and after we say our own "Let there be"? Even within the space of a single day, will it be possible to identify what our day was like until we recited the *Our Father* and what happened afterward?

THE CHRISTIAN IS A HYPERBOLE IN THE WORLD

In fact, people are involved in many things. When he reaches this point in his commentary on the *Our Father*, Abbé Pierre says more or less this: "Only a person who has lost his or her head can say such a thing, because it is to yield up one's trumps, to compromise one's ability, to open doors to let in a wind that will make everything topsy turvy; it is to provide a banquet for someone who is famished, namely, God, for Someone famished for love. To say 'Let there be' is to open wide the doors of our lives to Someone who wants everything. Faith has dimensions which completely do away with prudence and good sense."

God's will cannot be done without us. There is an acceptance, there is this leap of faith that depends on our freedom. We have to say, and to mean to the full, "Thy will be done." To pray is always to plan for something to happen. We have had the first Creation, we have had the second Creation, with the Lord's Redemption. And today we need have no doubt that a new Creation is about to happen. Today, in the Spirit, a new Creation is taking place. The world is the same, because that is how we want it. God gives us everything in order to recreate the world infinitely, beginning with what is closest to us. God opens new doors in this world through our cooperation with his will. Just as Mary who, through her availability, made God unexpectedly physically present in human history, it is for us too to exchange God "for pennies," to bring Him out into the open, show Him, present Him once again. Far too often, we remain attached to what is old, to the old creature that, as Saint Paul says, "persists within us." We forget that "the creation waits with eager longing for the revealing of the sons of God" (Rom 8:19).

What is God's will? God's will is Love. Our only duty is Love. And, when people say, "Thy will be done," they know beforehand that this means, "Let Love be fulfilled, made present, redesigned." In this sense, Paul of Tarsus is a man who leaves the orbit (of his culture and his age). Having been brought up in accordance with the Jewish law and attaching great importance to a legalistic, rigid, and intransigent observance of the law, when he discovers Jesus Christ he loses his foothold (or what he believed to be his foothold) completely. We cannot possibly follow him without ourselves taking into account the immensity of his interpretation of the Christian event. This is so in the Hymn to Love in 1 Corinthians 13, which he introduces with these words: "I will show you a still more excellent way [literally, I will show you a hyperbolic way!]" (1 Cor 12:31). In fact, the Christian is called to become a hyperbole in the world. The Pauline text provides us with a map: "If I speak in the tongues of men and of angels, but have not love, I am a noisy gong or a clanging cymbal. And if I have prophetic powers, and understand all mysteries and all knowledge, and if I have all faith, so as to remove mountains, but have not love, I am nothing. If I give away all I have, and if I deliver my body to be burned, but have not love, I gain nothing. [...] Love never ends; as for prophecies, they will pass away; as for tongues, they will cease; as for knowledge, it will pass away. [...] Faith, hope and love abide, but the greatest of these is love."

Think back on the story told by the Desert Fathers:

> A disciple went to see his teacher full of distress and almost ready to give it all up, and confessed to him: "My practice of meditation is a disaster. Either I get completely distracted, or my legs ache, or I fall asleep."
> "It will pass," his teacher told him calmly.
> A week later, the same disciple returned to his teacher, but this time full of joy:
> "My practice of meditation has become delightful! I feel so alert and so at peace. It is simply marvellous."
> The master replied as calmly as before: "This too will pass."

Saint Paul goes to the root of things: "All things will pass away." Except for love, or charity. In that case, let this love be put before us as a program, priority, urgent. A love which calls us to love, not with our heart but with the heart of God. When our own will opens itself to the will of God, love becomes life's silent symphony, its humble and abundant manifestation, its perfume. Even when we know that true love is crucifying. By loving, we will not amass riches, we shall certainly remain poorer; we shall grow older more quickly, we wear ourselves out, we lose ourselves. The measure of love is to give without measure. It is nonsense to suppose that love has a timetable, a spell of duty, a ticket office. Anyone who loves is ever alert, has antennae, sensors, eyes that do not grow accustomed to, nor do they give in to, a lack of love. As Fernando Pessoa used to say: "Sad is the person who is content!"

We are capable of this. We can say daringly, "Thy will be done on earth as it is in heaven," because God fills us with an overflowing measure of Love. And He says repeatedly to us: "Love Me as you are, from moment to moment and in the situation in which you find yourself, whether full of fervor or dryness, faithful or unfaithful. If you wait to become perfect first before you begin to love Me, you will never begin to love Me. There is only one thing that I will not grant, that you never love Me. Love Me as you are. I want your tattered heart, your needy gaze, your poor and empty hands. I love you to the depth of your weakness. I love the love of the poor. I want to see love, and only love, grow in the depth of your wretchedness. If, in order to love Me, you first wait to be perfect, you will never love Me. Love Me as you are!"

"Thy will be done, Lord." Let me be poor in your hands, let me not be afraid of my tattered heart, of my needy gaze, of my poor and empty hours. May I trust in love, may I live "within love, until it is only possible to love everything / and for everything to be found within love" (Herberto Hélder).

WE STILL HAVE A CHILDHOOD TO LIVE

If we look at the puzzle of the birth of Jesus, even in the restrained terms in which it is presented in the Gospels, we realize that there is nothing rosy about it. What those involved undergo is very much a story of instability, upset, and dismay. "What has happened to us?" Mary and Joseph must often have asked themselves, but also the shepherds who woke with a start and the wise men who had come from far away. "What has happened to us?" And, unlike ourselves, they had no comforting replies to hand, but a journey that was suggested to them out of the blue, in patient endurance and in confidence. Even the place where all this happened, a very lowly earthen-floor shelter for animals, clearly reveals the implacable hardness of the circumstances. But, had things been different, how could this divine story have served as a model for all human histories?

The birth of Jesus, the mystery of his Incarnation, radically alters the human condition because it inserts creative possibilities into it. We are accustomed to seeing in the unchanging cycle of the seasons—spring, summer, autumn, winter—the model of our own lives. We feel we have reached, all the more so each time, a spring or a summer that we thought would never emerge from the darkness of autumn or the grim emptiness of the winter landscape. However, the human birth of God brings to fruition a counter-cycle full of hope: our life ceases to find its explanation solely as a progression from birth to death, becoming instead an image of eternal rebirth. As we contemplate the manger in which the God child lay, however old we may be and whatever the burden of our years, we feel that the verse spoken by Pedro Homem de Mello is true of ourselves too: "my [our] childhood is not dead." In fact, childhood is not a nostalgic period in the past that is now closed, but the future that a new way of understanding history is opening out before us. We still have a childhood to live.

9

OUR LIVES ARE FED ON A LIFE SHARED

"Give Us This Day Our Daily Bread"

In a hyper-technological and sophisticated world such as ours, it is astonishing to realize the symbolic power that simple things continue to possess. Think about bread, for instance. Its appeal and meaning appear in many cultures and across many generations. Bread has become an extraordinary and universal symbol. It was so for our grandparents, it is so for ourselves. I remember when I was small that, if some bread fell off the table, we used to pick it up and kiss it, even if we could not eat it. Beyond the weight of what it symbolized, bread was, in itself, sacred. I think this is so because bread is a concrete expression of our humanity. Bread is not merely flour, yeast, water, and salt. It is much more than this. Bread is a sign of what is essential for life, of everything on which our survival depends, and without which we could not exist. It represents the threads that bind us to life and that keep us here on earth. That explains why we keep discovering in it an ever-widening meaning.

Bread also conveys the idea of sharing, communion, fellowship. To have only one loaf and be able to divide it into individual portions, to take pieces from a single loaf in order to feed the various guests seated around a table. Bread is not only bread. It is also the visible sign of the art of togetherness. At the root of words which are so dear to us such as *company, companion, companionship,* we have the Latin word for bread, *panis,* the *com-panis,* the act of eating the same bread [*panis*]. To say to someone, "You are the companion of my life," means that there is a sharing of food, of what gives life, and also of life, which makes us co-workers with God, and co-designers of creation. We use the expression "breadwinner." Bread is something vital in our lives.

At times, we spend our time asking God for secondary things, for mere trinkets and froth. And our prayer is trapped in our day-to-day lives....And we often forget to place God in the midst of our struggles, of our search for that which we need much more urgently. We can ask ourselves: "Am I to ask God for bread? If I don't work, it is not God who will give me bread. What I need to ask God for is for those things that I cannot acquire by my own efforts!" But what Jesus teaches us is that we are to ask God for the things that we can acquire by our own efforts or, in other words, to ask Him to impart a different meaning to what we can achieve and to make it really and truly necessary.

Jesus teaches us to ask God, to ask the Father, for the bread not to be mere bread, pure materiality, but that our bread should speak, become a kind of sacrament, an expression of all that, deep down, we are seeking and that the Lord is giving us, even in spiritual terms. We must ask God that our bread may bring about unity and not division, that our bread may be really and truly "Bread," a place where people can sit down together and not, as so often happens, those occasions when bread becomes the very thing that discriminates and is a cause of separation. To ask God that our bread may celebrate is to show our gratitude to God and our love for others.

To ask God that "our daily bread" may be good not only for our stomach, but also for our heart and soul. That is to say, that the bread can acquire such a human meaning that it becomes divine. That what we are constructing day by day possesses a transcendent meaning and is not merely something dumb that has no power of speech. That work is not merely a mechanical and obligatory activity but that one senses something more in it: the love of God, the heart of God, the life of God.

We pray "our daily bread" because it is a sad state of affairs when I alone have bread. It is then a bread that it is difficult to swallow. Bread eaten alone has only half the taste, only a far-thing's worth of joy. We ask God for **our** bread, the bread of all, the bread for all.

One of the oldest images of the Church, preserved in the *Didache*, depicts it as follows: "Even as these grains of wheat were scattered over the hills, and were gathered together and became a single loaf, so let Your Church be gathered together from the ends of the earth into Your kingdom." To ask for "our bread" is to ask for this fellowship. It is to ask not only for my own harvest, but for all harvests. And it is to commit oneself to kneading a single loaf, capable of feeding both myself and others.

ASK FOR HUNGER FOR THOSE WHO HAVE BREAD

There is a paraphrase of this petition of the *Our Father* that always makes me shudder, as it reminds me of the extent to which it makes us all responsible. It is a line of poetry written by José Agostinho Batista that goes as follows: "Our daily bread which you do not give me today."

The *Our Father* is a prayer that binds, a prayer of commit-ment, including political commitment in the world; it is not only intimate and personal. If I pray the *Our Father*, I must pray that there may be bread for all, for those close to me and for those far away. To pray the *Our Father* is to assume responsibility for the state of the world. In the Emmaus Communities founded by Abbé Pierre, the following prayer is recited at the table: "Lord, help us to obtain bread for those who are hungry and to ensure hunger for those who have bread." To find bread for those who are hungry....To seek what is essential to life, whether material or spiritual. To ensure hunger for those who have bread...for those who are satisfied, who live in their own little glass case oblivious of others, for those who could do something and do not do it, for those who never thought of the *Our Father* as a prayer that necessarily propels us toward fellowship. Bread is a symbol of this fellowship. It is not merely the result of fellowship, but must provoke it, re-invent it.

Nowadays, there is a tradition (which is really a spiritual tool) that has almost become obsolete and that would be good to bring back into circulation, namely, the practice of *fasting*. We live with the minced-up digestion that the world has made of us. Very quickly our *Being* is relegated and is replaced by the rush to *Have*. We rush from one place to another, as if we were hostages and tools rather than independent and creative beings. Now, fasting (for example, to eat less or abstain from overeating, to waste less, to criticize less, and so on) amounts to a spiritual act, as it widens the field of our freedom. Without realizing it, there are so many currents that we are caught up in, and so many forms of subjection that reduce our capacity to enter into fellowship with others. To fast, to adopt a more frugal way of living, creates new availabilities, makes possible a better practice of discernment, even improves our sense of humor...and prepares us to enter into a sharing solidarity with the very poor.

PRAISING THE PROVISIONAL

We pray, "Give us this day our daily bread," the bread for each day. When the people left Egypt and embarked on their forty years of wandering in the desert as far as Mount Sinai, they were given every day a portion of bread which was the manna, but they only ever received enough for each day. Let us have another look at the text:

> When the dew had gone up, there was on the face of the wilderness a fine, flake-like thing, fine as hoarfrost on the ground. When the people of Israel saw it they said to one another: "What is it?" For they did not know what it was. And Moses said to them, "It is the bread which the Lord has given you to eat." This is what the Lord has commanded: "Gather of it, every man of you, as much as he can eat; you shall take an omer apiece, according to the number of persons whom each of you has in his tent." And the people of Israel did so; they gathered, some more, some less. But when they measured it with an omer, he that gathered much had nothing over, and he that gathered little had no lack; each gathered according to what he could eat. And Moses said to them, "Let no man leave any of it till the morning." But they did not listen to Moses; some left part of it till the morning, and it bred worms and became foul; and Moses was angry with them. Morning by morning they gathered it, each as much as he could eat. (Exod 16:14–21)

When we are walking we cannot carry unduly heavy weights, as otherwise we shall not get very far. The traveler and the pilgrim have to be prepared to learn how to live on what one has each day. This is what living in God means. Every day we have God. Hence, we cannot do what the man in the parable did, for he filled his barns with bread and then said to himself: "Now, my soul, your barns are full so you can relax." Relax your vigilance. But the Lord said: "Foolish fellow, this day the Lord will come in search of your soul, and what will you have to show in His presence?"

If we want to be God's nomads, if we want to live in Him, we must establish a great freedom in relation to things. The truth is that they imprison us. What we possess very quickly comes to possess us. For the Christian, a frugal life style bears better witness than a thousand words to one's faith in God. We have been plunged into a time when everything impels us toward competition...where the superfluous is foisted onto us as being absolutely necessary for our happiness.

The Gospel teaches us not to heap up but to multiply. Jesus shows us the possibilities for life hidden in a single loaf. With a single loaf we can do much, if we learn the art of multiplying life, of multiplying generosity, solidarity, tenderness, the ability to suffer with others and of putting ourselves in the place of others....We are assailed by doubt: am I obliged to give, maybe I ought not to give, am I giving people bad habits, what if...and it is true that we do have to ask ourselves these questions. To give something to a beggar automatically may be a way of getting rid of him. "Here you are! Now go!" What did Jesus do when he multiplied the loaves? "He said to them, 'How many loaves have you? Go and see.' And when they had found out, they said, 'Five and two fish.' Then he commanded them all to sit down by companies upon the green grass. So they sat down in groups, by hundreds and fifties. And taking the five loaves and two fish he looked up to heaven, and blessed and broke the loaves, and gave them to the disciples to set before the people; and he divided the two fish among them all" (Mark 6:38–41). Table fellowship is to eat with others, to share the basics, to share life, conversation, tenderness, to prolong being with others.

ALL LIVES ARE BREAD

All lives can be fitted into the daily, almost trivial image of bread that is broken and shared. For lives are things that are sown, that grow, mature, are harvested, made into a dough just as bread is. For not only do we savor and consume the world but, within ourselves, we perceive that the world, that time, in turn consumes us, wears us out, devours us. For good reasons and for bad ones, no one remains untouched. We are a lump of dough that can be divided up into pieces, the soft center of bread that is made into breadcrumbs, a thickness that slowly disappears.

The question is to know with what awareness, with what intention, with what intensity we live this inevitable process. We all wear out, undoubtedly. But in doing what? We all feel that life is fleeting. But how to turn this tragic fact into a form of fruitful affirmation and itself full of life?

For this reason, we are astonished by Jesus' words that are recalled in every Eucharist. He took the bread and said: "Take and eat ye all of this as this bread is my body given for you." The Eucharist, which is sometimes repeated as if it were merely a devout ritual, a routine sign of a belonging, is, in fact, the vital place of decision about what makes life. All lives are bread, but not all are Eucharist, that is, a radical offering of self, commitment, gift, service. All lives come to an end, but not all go to the end in giving birth to this (human and divine) vitality which is inscribed in them. It is of these things that the Eucharist speaks.

Jesus is our bread, and when we pray "Give us this day our daily bread," we are asking the Father to give us Jesus, to bring us Jesus. "And Jesus said to them: 'Truly, truly, I say to you, it was not Moses who gave you the bread from heaven; my Father gives you the true bread from heaven. For the bread of God is that which comes down from heaven, and gives life to the world.' They said to him, 'Lord, give us this bread always!' Jesus said to them, 'I am the bread of life; he who comes to me shall not hunger, and he who believes in me shall never thirst'" (John 6:27–35).

Let us feed one another. We are here for one another, whether listening or speaking, in silence or in laughter, in giving and in loving, a necessary food, because our lives are nourished with life (and a life that is shared).

10

GOD HAS FAITH IN US
"Forgive Us Our Trespasses"

I remember a film of Nanni Moretti's, I think it was *The Son's Room*, in which one of the characters, who is living through a period of deep mourning, begins putting the teacups away in a cupboard. As she does so, she realizes that one of the cups is cracked down one side. She tries to hide the crack, placing the cup so that only the uncracked side is visible. But she knows that that particular cup lacks something. That cup is the symbol of her life, of all our lives, consisting of losses, gaps, and disintegrations that we cannot hide. There is a wholeness that collapses, a unity that is broken, a happiness that corrodes, fades away.

It is true that one can do all in one's power not to think. We live in a time marked by automatism and the illusion is created that life can be resolved by pressing a button. We open a door by pressing a button and the door opens; to turn on a light, for any kind of task, whether simple or complex, all we have to do is to press something and what we want to happen happens. It is all very quick, immediate, painless, requiring a minimum of effort, with no bother and no sacrifice. With a minimum of effort, we keep life going on the surface. More and more, consumer goods are presented to us as substitutes for the human paths that we have no choice but to follow. We need only to look carefully at all those advertisements that assail us at all times: "Buy car X—

you will feel like a new man [or woman], full of courage, fulfilled at last," when we know that courage and fulfillment are the result of paths we have chosen, choices we have made, a patient maturing with ups and downs, progress and retreat....No, merely buying a new car is not enough to make us feel like that, nor is buying a sophisticated perfume enough to make a person attractive; nor yet a new vacuum cleaner or washing machine....

The great danger is to allow ourselves to get involved in an inauthentic life, a life that is not a real life, consisting in images and appearances. What becomes important in such a life is basically the illusion that one projects and that has to be preserved at all costs. Nowadays, many people seem more interested in keeping up appearances than in saving themselves. In an ever-growing vacuum, the imitation ends up obscuring the original. And we are witnessing the triumph of a "show" society, governed by a provisional and functional ethic that does not actually touch people themselves. The great life questions are handed over to the market strategy, to those who advise on image presentation and etiquette. The human adventure has become an adventure inside a capsule or a simulator and does not manage to become a history that is really exposed to what it is. Hence, there are many people who, while living continually in experiencing sensations, say: "Oh, if only I could at least manage to feel something." The great question is this: "Shall I be able to do it?" "Having offended against life, shall I be able to get back to being reconciled to living it?"

SOMEONE IS WATCHING US WITH HOPE

We need someone to watch over us with hope. Michelangelo used to say that his sculptures were not the result of a process of invention but of liberation. He would look at the rough stone, completely untouched, and could see what it could turn into. For this reason, in describing his work, the sculptor used to say: "What I do is to set things free." I am convinced that the great works of creation (including that of the creation and the re-creation of human beings) are the result of a similar process, for which I can find no better expression than this: an exercise of hope. Without hope, all we can see is the stone, the rough block, the tiring wearisome and irremovable obstacle. It is hope that begins opening the door, making visible, beyond the difficulties, the richness of as yet hidden possibilities. Hope is capable of entering into dialogue with the future and bringing it closer. From beginning to end, our existence is the result of a profession of faith.

All things and each one of us is a way, an experience of incompleteness, of lingering in the as yet unfinished. The hardness and opacity of stone. Masterpieces do not spring from spontaneous generation. They are the fruit of this patient and very slow gestation that we ourselves are in. But, without hope, without this act of creation, this act of love, there will be no masterpiece. Each of Michelangelo's works undoubtedly needed carefully selected marble, but also much hope. The marble could be of better or poorer quality, as is clear from the famous unfinished sculptures of slaves that are on display in the Louvre. But it is hope that can never diminish. In the smallest as in the largest things, we find the same summons to hope. In what is perhaps the most beautiful poem on hope, Charles Péguy says: "The faith that I love best is hope."

GOD BELIEVES IN ALL HUMAN BEINGS

One day, the prophet Jeremiah, too, went to reflect on the work of a creative artist: "The word that came to Jeremiah from the Lord: 'Arise, and go down to the potter's house, and there I will let you hear my words.' So I went down to the potter's house, and there he was working at his wheel. And the vessel he was making of clay was spoiled in the potter's hand, and he reworked it into another vessel, as it seemed good to the potter to do" (Jer 18:1–4). "He reworked it." God is the potter, the One who does not throw out the clay in spite of the misshapen forms. It has been like that since the beginning. "The Lord formed man of dust from the ground, and breathed into his nostrils the breath of life; and man became a living being" (Gen 2:7). The God of the Bible refuses to abandon man. Even when He recognizes the extreme fragility in which our freedom is built up ("Your love is like a morning cloud, like the dew that goes early away" [Hos 6:4]). He does not cease believing, trusting, hoping ("How can I give you up, O Ephraim? How can I hand you over, O Israel? My heart recoils within me, my compassion grows warm and tender I will not execute my fierce anger..." [Hos 11:8–9]). I think, too, of the lovely title of Hans Urs von Balthasar's book *God Has Hope for All*. We are unceasingly shaped by this hope multiplied *ad infinitum* by this readiness for the loving recreation of God's own work. Yet another quote from the Book of Hosea: "Therefore, behold, I will allure her, and bring her into the wilderness, and speak tenderly to her. And there I will give her her vineyards, and make the Valley of Achor a door of hope. And there she shall answer as in the days of her youth" (Hos 2:14–15). God takes the liberating initiative. He sees, He hears the human situation. He comes to meet us in order to liberate us; to pluck us out of the land of exile, from a life that is no life, cut off due to slavery. God has compassion on the reality of our situation. He releases and saves real solid people who have the courage to take on the solidity of their lives as they actually are, in all their difficulties, problems, and limitations that turn us into the playthings of countless forms of slavery. God does not save what we seem to be, what we pretend to be. He saves the person that we are, because it is in this that He believes, it is this He loves. This profound liberation that God brings about by his forgiveness is thus a real recreation, an unceasing call to life. Once I saw the words "Do you believe in life before death?" scribbled on a wall. It shook me. Obviously, to believe in life after death widens the horizon tremendously. However, if for some reason or other, I cease to believe in life (that is, the possibility of a real life) before I die, everything becomes peculiar, dark, and lost. God does not abandon people.

LET US LEARN TO FORGIVE IN THE LOVE WITH WHICH WE OURSELVES ARE LOVED

"See what love the Father has given us," urges the author of the First Letter of Saint John (3:1). Only those who experience the extraordinary power of love can perceive the need for forgiveness. It is those who discover how God has always been at their side, how He embraced them when they fell, and is leading them forward toward greater strength, who possess a greater commitment to love. We need to place ourselves within the mystery of love in order to perceive the meaning and extent of forgiveness. We tend to do too much calculating, to keep withdrawing, adding, subtracting, reaching conclusions…whereas, in fact, the mystery of forgiveness is experienced quite simply in love. There must first gush forth the realization that one is loved, and it is this which opens us to the need, and the desire, for God's forgiveness. Saint Paul makes this very clear in his Letter to the Romans, by detaching forgiveness from any sense of merit. The offer of forgiveness reveals the gratuitousness of love, how unlimited it is. "For there is no distinction; since all have sinned and fall short of the glory of God, they are justified by his grace as a gift, through the redemption which is in Christ Jesus" (Rom 3:22–24).

Some of Jesus' encounters with people are exemplary. He is the Master of forgiveness, because he introduces love precisely into those hearts where the impossibility of loving, an irremediable failure to believe, had taken root: "He entered Jericho and was passing through. And there was a man named Zacchaeus; he was a chief tax collector, and rich. And he sought to see who Jesus was, but could not, on account of the crowd, because he was small of stature. So he ran on ahead and climbed up into a sycamore tree to see him, for he was to pass that way. And when Jesus came to the place, he looked up and said to him, 'Zacchaeus, make haste and come down; for I must stay at your house today.' So he made haste and came down, and received him joyfully. And when they saw it they all murmured, 'He has gone in to be the guest of a man who is a sinner.' And Zacchaeus stood and said to the Lord, 'Behold, Lord, the half of my goods I give to the poor; and if I have defrauded any one of anything, I restore it fourfold.' And Jesus said to him, 'Today salvation has come to this house, since he also is a son of Abraham. For the Son of Man came to seek and to save the lost'" (Luke 19:5–10). Zacchaeus' transformation was triggered by the display of an immense and undeserved love which Jesus, against all expectations, placed before him.

"O the depth of the riches and wisdom and knowledge of God!" (Rom 11:33).

And let us believe that God does not wish to give us anything other than his forgiveness. He does not wish to give us anything else! The image of God conveyed to us by Jesus is that of a forgiving Father. Just think of the scandal Jesus provoked by telling his parable about the prodigal son (Luke 15:11–32). Jesus was talking to fathers of families, people who knew very well how to bring up their children. How come that, when that out-and-out rascal who leaves home and wastes all his possessions returns, he is treated like a king's son! God's knowledge is that of forgiveness. The son is still a long way off and the father rushes out to meet him. He makes the approach. He breaks into the apologetic speech of the son in which he was asking to be allowed to remain and be treated as one of the servants. But the father "embraces him and kisses him," that is, he makes him lovable, and reassures him: "Bring quickly the best robe, and put it on him; and put a ring on his hand, and shoes on his feet; and bring the fatted calf and kill it, and let us eat and make merry; for this my son was dead, and is alive again: he was lost, and is found" (Luke 15:22–24). We shall not know what this is unless we can feel, really and unconditionally, that God does the same for ourselves.

Faced with the signs of lack of love in ourselves, the scratches of our offenses, the ruptures of suffering, only an excess of love (and forgiveness is precisely this, an excess of love) can restore the oneness of the image and likeness to God in ourselves. Only the excess of love makes it possible to understand forgiveness. This unforeseeable pardon, this unconditional and measureless pardon, this is the pardon that is capable of lifting us to our feet.

The *Our Father* is the great school of forgiveness. Whenever we pray it, we always encounter the invitation to plunge into the Mystery of God's forgiveness, in an incalculable sea of love.

11

A UNILATERAL DECISION TO LOVE

"...As We Forgive Those Who Trespass Against Us"

The parallel that this phrase of the *Our Father* establishes with the preceding one is not in terms of a business deal according to which if God forgives us, then we will forgive others. This would be a kind of swap: we will only give if God gives to us. There is, in fact, a parallelism between this invocation of the *Our Father* and the preceding one. But only in the sense that we accept that it is God who is the source and master of all forgiveness and it is in his image and likeness that we are learning to forgive.

Granting forgiveness is not something that comes to us spontaneously. The statement "we forgive" has to do with the circulation of God in us. It has to do with the gift of being children of God. The German mystic Angelus Silesius wrote: "We do not know what God is. He is neither light, nor spirit, nor truth, nor unity, nor what we call divinity; neither is He wisdom, reason, love, goodness, or any other thing; still less is He non-existence, or essence or affection. He is what neither I, nor you, nor any creature has ever experienced, except by becoming what God himself is." What God is, we do not know. He is a mystery that our knowledge cannot unravel. Anything we may say about God is always an approximation. Because, in fact, we only know what

God is by ourselves becoming what God is. And forgiveness is pre-eminently one of the places in which we experience what God is.

WHAT FORGIVENESS IS NOT

It might be useful to begin by stating what forgiveness is not.

Forgiveness is not merely to make excuses. To make excuses for someone is one thing, to forgive is quite another. To make excuses for someone is something rational; it is to look at someone who has upset us and try to understand the reasons and the preconditioning underlying that person's behavior. In this way, even in the case of extreme violence, the action of the person who committed the offense can to some extent be attenuated/mitigated (he or she experienced serious problems in childhood, did not have the opportunities other people have had, feels isolated and deprived of a stable protective environment…). This is to make excuses. It is the rational search for reasons that can cast some kind of light on the offense committed. But it is not yet forgiveness. We can and we must make excuses for others, but we must also recognize that forgiveness is something quite different.

Equally, to forgive is not simply to forget. We often confuse the two things and we say, "Oh, I can't forget," as if this necessarily meant "I cannot bring myself to forgive." No. Forgiveness is one thing, forgetting another. This is so because there are some things that it is impossible to forget. That does not depend entirely on anything that we ourselves can do. There are offenses that leave such indelible marks that we cannot forget them, even if we wish to do so. And if we do forget them at the conscious level, they remain in our unconscious and, as a result, manifest themselves in gestures and reactions. The question we need to ask ourselves is this: "Can I forgive an offense that I am not going to be able to forget?" And, however impossible it may seem (since, in fact, it comes from a revelation begotten from neither flesh nor blood), the reply is this: "Yes, I can forgive" precisely because forgiveness is something different from forgetting or from memory.

Forgiveness is also not to administer justice. There are situations in which justice, when faced with them, has no alternative but to condemn. We all know that this is so. But the solution of granting forgiveness is different. This is why there are pictures of people who have been condemned to death being visited by a priest who grants them forgiveness. They are going to die because of an interpretation of justice, but forgiveness can keep open for them, even at the last moment, the gates of life. Forgiveness has nothing at all to do with the irremediable.

Forgiveness is also not a declaration of moral superiority. We may seem to be being magnanimous and generous, but what in fact is it that we are doing? We are tying up the person with what we are giving them: "You didn't deserve it, but I gave it to you....Now, take care." We must be careful not to turn our forgiveness into a form of power or arbitrariness that closes us off even more.

WHAT IS FORGIVENESS?

Forgiveness is to be ready not to place the emphasis either on the person who has been offended or on the person who committed the offence....Argumentation leads to a paralyzing impasse, in which we can live for many years. Forgiveness, on the other hand, introduces the relational figure of a triangle by bringing the God factor into the picture, namely, the possibility of actually living the love that we contemplate in God. Forgiveness is not a matter between two people; three are involved. Basically, to forgive is to say: "It is true that this offense was aggressive, it injured my being, it is something that I cannot forgive completely, that I shall probably not be able to forget so quickly or even at all…but I do not want to stop loving Love; I want to distance myself from the reactive logic of violence." Love alone is capable of healing. When all is said and done, it is only by making present what God is in my life, only by "becoming what God is" that I can overcome the blockage of evil. Forgiveness is not something that I create in myself. It is something that I allow God to bring about in me. It is allowing God to enter into my history and his logic to become mine.

In order to be able to forgive, I have to lay my relationship with the other before another, namely, God. And I must try to ensure that it is God's way of seeing things that predominates. Doing this will give me strength so that, having been the victim of an offense of some kind, I can reach a unilateral decision of love. The other will not become hostage to my forgiveness, because, basically, I am not granting forgiveness to a concrete person, or only to that person, but I am bringing the life of God into my own life and into the way the world works. And there is no further need for me to remind the other of the offense committed. The only thing God asks of us is that we remember the forgiveness.

When commenting on that Gospel passage in which Jesus said, "Come to me all you who labor and are heavy laden, and I will give you rest. Take my yoke upon you, and learn from me; for I am gentle and lowly in heart and you will find rest for your souls. For my yoke is easy and my burden is light" (Matt 11:28–30), Kierkegaard explained that the light yoke spoken of by Jesus is the yoke of forgiveness and our own heavy yoke is the yoke of offenses that have not been forgiven.

God does not want us to dwell on the memory of past offenses. At times, to remember past sins is a temptation to dwell on sin itself in all its enigmatic and endless convolutions. Even a scruple, taken to the extreme, can be a devious way of holding onto what we need to purify. Evangelical wisdom commands us to shake the dirt and dust completely from our feet.

What the Lord keeps on saying is "Remember forgiveness." It is as having ourselves been forgiven and forgiving others that we are called to live. Forgiveness is a "light yoke." We must, of course, endeavor to develop the potentialities that are concealed by forgiveness. Even if we are the fruit of a formation that lays great stress on the weight of sin, it seems to me that the great conversion consists in emphasizing the light of God's forgiveness in our lives.

There is that story of the two monks who, as they were about to cross a stream, met a woman who asked one or the other of them to carry her across on their shoulders. It was a totally unlooked-for request and was against their rule. But there and then the younger of the two stooped down and carried the woman over to the other side. The woman expressed her thanks, and the monks continued on their way. The older of the two monks, however, spent the entire journey in rebuking the younger one: "What a thing to do!" "Fancy doing a thing like that!" "You know the rule...." In the end, the younger monk could stand it no longer and replied: "Look. I carried the woman from one bank to the other and then left her. You, however, have carried her all the way here."

Let us start from our condition of having been forgiven....There is no doubt that to understand this is to place ourselves in the school of the Gospel. When we live in forgiveness, we really begin to make progress in the way of growing in knowledge of God and the following of Jesus. Not in any abstract way, but concretely and deliberately. Forgiveness opens doors within us. And then we cease to carry yesterday's burdens in order to discover the wings we need for today.

There are some stories which convey to us better than a cupboard full of concepts the power of reparation that we are seeking. Here are just three:

The first was told by the Jewish writer and Nobel Peace Prize–winner Elie Wiesel. As a child, he was a prisoner in Auschwitz with his parents, his brothers, sisters, and friends. He alone survived. We can imagine the extent to which he felt himself stripped of everything. From 1945 onward, when the war was over, years went by in which his only aim in life was to seek an impossible justice for what was utterly irremediable. "How could such horror be possible?…How could it have happened?" And this was his life. Every day he fell asleep and woke up in hell. He could not find his soul. Until, in the end, he went to talk to a rabbi. And the rabbi said to him: "My son, as long as you cannot forgive, you will continue to be a prisoner in Auschwitz." It was this word that wrought a permanent change in his heart.

The second is not exactly a story. It is a prayer, one of the most beautiful prayers that I know. It was found among the things left behind by a Jew, who in fact had died in a concentration camp. This is the prayer: "Lord, when You come in your glory, do not remember only the men of good will, remember also those of evil will. And, on the Day of Judgment, do not remember only the cruelties and violence that they inflicted on others: remember, too, the fruits that we have produced on account of the things they did to us. Remember the patience, the courage, the sense of fellowship, the humility, the greatness of soul and fidelity that our executioners ended up awakening in each one of us. Grant, then, Lord, that the fruits brought forth in us may serve also for the salvation of these men."

And here is the third story: A woman called Ann went into a bakery in a shopping center to order a cake for her son's birthday. As any one of us would have done, she left her name and telephone number. On the very morning of the boy's birthday, he was run over by a car, went into a coma, and eventually died. The baker had no idea what had happened. All he knew was that the woman had ordered a cake that she had not come to collect. So as day followed day, he began to persecute her with anonymous telephone calls. The woman eventually realized who it was who was doing the telephoning and, traumatized by her grief for the death of her son, she decided to go at once, with her husband, to the shopping center in order to teach him a lesson. It was very early in the morning so the shop was closed, but the baker was in the actual bakery behind the shop, making bread. At the beginning of the encounter, all one could see was the anger of the woman and the resentment of the baker. But when Ann told him what he did not know, the anger dwindled and gave way to something else.

"Let me say how sorry I am," the baker said, putting his elbows on the table. "God alone knows how sorry. Listen to me. I'm just a baker. I don't claim to be anything else....That don't excuse my doing what I did, I know that. But I'm deeply sorry....You got to understand: what it comes down to is I don't know how to act anymore. Please, let me ask you if you can find it in your hearts to forgive me?"

It was warm inside the bakery. Ann and her husband took off their coats. The baker placed some cups on the table. They sat down. And although they were very tired and in anguish, they listened to what the baker had to say.

"You probably need to eat something," he said. "I hope you will eat some hot rolls I have made myself. You must eat in order to cope with the situation. Eating can be a comfort in a situation like this," he said.

They went on listening to him. Then they slowly ate dark fresh-smelling bread that the man cut for them, and they were surprised at its healing and delicate taste. As the morning wore on, they remained on there in conversation. The fluorescent lights in the shopping center were slowly replaced by the light of the early morning that began to pour in through the windows.

I love this story by Raymond Carver. It says a lot in a short space. The words create an atmosphere of welcome and listening. The food (and it is no accident that the food is bread) brings healing, dries tears. Within the people involved, a kind of resurrection takes place. Forgiveness in fact opens us to an understanding of the paschal mystery.

12

THE FOURTH TEMPTATION
"...And Lead Us not Into Temptation"

In one of her remarks well-seasoned with humor, Saint Teresa of Avila tells us that it is foolish to suppose that "souls with whom God communicates in what would seem to be a privileged way are, however, reassured by this to such an extent that they need no longer fear or weep for their sins." In fact, we are called to live the gift of God right to the end, in frailty, in weakness, in trust and in temptation. The problems that beset us may vary in kind, in frequency, or in intensity, but they will certainly be always with us. There will always be temptations. What changes, in the course of a process of human and spiritual growth to maturity, is the way in which we cope with these things. It is by discerning the nature of our temptations that we often come to understand our own individuality and difference, the real impact of life in ourselves, our underlying reality and its unreadable vestiges. Temptation makes us human. It is a way. Saint Paul begged the Lord three times to release him from the thorn in his flesh (2 Cor 12:9). But in vain! The reply he received was: "My grace is sufficient for you, for my power is made perfect in weakness" (2 Cor 12:9).

Meister Eckhart explains the "great benefit and usefulness" of temptations: they make us fight a continual battle; force us to be constantly on the watch; even when they humiliate us, they keep us centered on God.

It is exactly this: the dream of perfection may well be a pathway that we skim over or an illusion that prevents us from penetrating to the true and paradoxical state of life. It takes us so long to get rid of our mania for things to be perfect and free from fear of the real, and to cure ourselves of the impulse that isolates us in the comfort of idealizations, or overcome the vice of superimposing on reality a whole series of false images! Thomas Merton wrote emotionally something that should make us all stop in our tracks: "The Christ that we discover really present within us is quite different from the One that we try in vain to admire and idolize in ourselves. On the contrary: He wished to become one with the person that we do not love in ourselves, because He took upon himself our wretchedness and our suffering, our poverty and our sins....We will never find peace if we listen to the blindness that tells us that the battle has been won. We will only find peace if we are capable of listening to and embracing the contradictory dance that throbs in our blood....It is here that one hears best the echoes of the victory of the Risen Christ."

Saint Paul understood this, because his response was: "I will all the more gladly boast of my weaknesses, that the power of Christ may rest upon me. For the sake of Christ, then, I am content with weaknesses, insults, hardships, persecutions, and calamities; for when I am weak, then I am strong" (2 Cor 12:9–10). Paul presents the Faith as a paradoxical hypothesis: when I am weak, then I am strong. Faith struggles and grows to maturity in times of need, distress, insults, suffering, that is, when one finds oneself assailed by temptation. There is no question of juggling with or overcoming this situation: it is within the experience that I am strong. It is, of course, a paradox. But that is where the real spiritual experience takes place.

The great obstacle to a godly life is not frailty or weakness but hardness and rigidity. It is not the vulnerability and the humiliation but their opposite: pride and self-sufficiency, self-justification, isolation, violence, the delirium of power. There is a poem by Lao Tsé that says: "When men are born they are weak and fragile. Death makes them hard and rigid. The grass and the trees when they first appear are weak and fragile. Death makes them squalid and dried up. The hard and the rigid lead to death. The weak and the flexible lead to life." The strength of what we really need, the grace that is so necessary to us, is not ours but Christ's. And it is he who gives us the example of embracing humanity entirely in all its drama, since it was "in his wounds that we were healed" (Isa 53:5).

THE FIRST THREE TEMPTATIONS

It is interesting to note that the text of the *Our Father* offers a clear (and mysterious) mirror effect in relation to another Gospel passage, namely, Jesus' temptations. The *Our Father* is a reply to this episode that is as literal as it is brimful of hope. Let us have another look at it: "Then Jesus was led up by the Spirit into the wilderness to be tempted by the devil. And he fasted forty days and forty nights, and afterwards he was hungry. And the tempter came and said to him, 'If you are the Son of God, command these stones to become loaves of bread.' But he answered, 'It is written, *Man shall not live by bread alone, but by every word that proceeds from the mouth of God.*' Then the devil took him to the holy city, and set him on the pinnacle of the temple, and said to him, 'If you are the Son of God, throw yourself down; for it is written: *He will give his angels charge of you and On their hands they will bear you up, lest you strike your foot against a stone.*' Jesus said to him, 'Again it is written: *You shall not tempt the Lord your God.*' Again the devil took him to a very high mountain, and showed him all the kingdoms of the world and the glory of them; and he said to him, 'All these I will give you, if you will fall down and worship me.' Then Jesus said to him,

'Begone, Satan! For it is written: *You shall worship the Lord your God and him only shall you serve.*' Then the devil left him and behold angels came and ministered to him" (Matt 4:1–11).

These temptations of Jesus did not all happen in a single day. They undoubtedly happened in the course of his life. We can only imagine the voices, the conflicting pressures, the contradictory signs, the dilemmas, the weight of the expectations which must have been brought to bear on Jesus. These three great formulations summarize all that Jesus endured and, at the same time, they indicate the intimate struggles that are common to the human condition.

Here the symbolism is important, beginning with the number of days for which Jesus withdrew: forty days, which correspond to the forty years during which the People of God wandered in the desert. Except that, whereas the People of the Old Covenant were incapable of giving a fully positive reply to God's gift, Jesus said a real "yes," a full and complete "yes" to the Father. Whereas our Desert Fathers, even when presented with God's gifts, were constantly denying Him, buried in their own lack of trust, Jesus always lived in a sincere, total, given, committed relationship. And this is the secret of Jesus' life. For this reason, he is the first fruit of a new people, the beginning of a re-created history. In fact, Jesus in no way exempted himself from any aspect of our humanity, but took it all on himself radically, in all its contradictions, paroxysms, and limitations. "Though he was in the form of God, he did not count equality with God a thing to be grasped, but emptied himself, taking the form of a servant, being born in the likeness of men" (Phil 2:6–7).

The three temptations of Jesus represent all those that surround and lay siege to ourselves:

- *The temptation to materialism*: to consume material things only, to make this the purpose of one's existence, forgetting the transcendent vocation of the human being. To idolize material things, and in our madness use them as a substitute for God Himself.

- *The temptation to providentialism*: to be forgetful of the human vocation. To refuse our own responsibility for history. To confuse our relationship with God with an imaginary and magic providentialism. We cannot throw ourselves down from the pinnacles of temples in the belief that God will bear us up. We must have a healthy respect for our limitations and do our share.
- *The temptation to absolutism*: to make an idol of our power, whatever it may be. To make of control and possession the source of our happiness. To see in this the horizon for the meaning of life. To lose the sense of adoration, that is, the experience of humble openness to what is greater than ourselves, to the infinity of God.

Jesus did not yield to temptation because he had, in fact, a very deep relationship with the Father. At every moment he lived in the Father's orbit. He lived as Son, at every moment, in every gesture, in all his attitudes, in every choice....God was God in him. Hence, fidelity to the Father enabled him to reinvent our humanity, which is so often blocked on account of these very temptations.

THE FOURTH TEMPTATION

"Who are you? I expected three visitors, not four." It was with a surprise such as this that the martyred Archbishop Thomas Becket greeted the visit paid to him by the "fourth tempter" in T. S. Eliot's well-known play *Murder in the Cathedral*. Thanks to his intelligence and courage, Thomas Becket, who was of lowly origin, had managed to achieve prominence in the world. He had gained the friendship and trust of the King of England, Henry II, who made him Chancellor. Everything changed, however, when the king, who had hoped to gain control of the Church through his Chancellor, appointed him Archbishop of Canterbury. Very quickly an irreconcilable conflict broke out between the spiritual and temporal powers. Being subjected to persecution, Thomas felt obliged to go into exile in France, where he was under papal protection. However, seven years later, he decided to return to be with his Christians. Eliot's play begins with Thomas's arrival in the Cathedral in Canterbury. He sought to occupy his place as shepherd of his people, but without sacrificing his spiritual freedom. The theme of the first act is the inner battles he has to fight. Three tempters appear, together with a fourth, unexpected and more terrifying than the other three, as this fourth one endeavors to show him that his desire to remain faithful is no more than pride and vanity in disguise. Thomas exclaims:

> Who are you, tempting me with my own desires?
> Others have come, temporal tempters,
> With pleasure and power at palpable price.
> What do you offer? What do you ask? […]
>
> Others offered real goods. Worthless
> But real. You only offer
>
> Dreams to damnation. […]
>
> Is there no way, in my soul's sickness
> Does not lead to damnation in pride?

As Simone Weil has said that the worst of temptations, indeed, "the only temptation for man is to be abandoned to his own resources in the presence of evil. His nothingness is then proved experimentally." Hence, it is the fourth temptation that radically undermines a person's confidence. It attacks one's roots, resulting in implosion by nihilism and lack of belief. Nothing is worth anything. We can trust in nothing. We cannot put our heart into anything that moves us, even when we are sincerely moving toward God. "And can we in fact put our trust in God?" the tempter whispers to us.

One of the most astonishing paraphrases of the *Our Father* in the whole of literature is the one spoken by a waiter in Ernest Hemingway's short story entitled "A Clean, Well-Lighted Place." The bar was one of those Spanish bars that are open until the early hours of the morning, and there were two waiters. One of them was, in effect, urging the customers to leave so that he could go home, albeit only a few minutes early, whereas the other waiter was in no hurry. He admitted: "I have never had confidence and I am not young. […] I am of those who like to stay late at the café….With all those who do not want to go to bed, with all those who need a light for the night." And as he wiped down the bar for the last time, he murmured to himself:

> Our nada who art in nada,
> nada be thy name
> thy kingdom nada
> thy will be nada
> in nada as it is in nada.
> Give us this nada our daily nada
> and nada us our nada
> as we nada our nadas
> and nada us not into nada
> but deliver us from nada.

"My God, my God, why have you forsaken me?" Jesus confronts not only the silence of men but also the seemingly invincible silence of God. The Cross is as disconcerting as an insuperable difficulty. We are called to contemplate the mystery of God and of Man in the most devastating silence the world has ever known. By his death, Jesus stooped to embrace all silences, even the abysmal ones, those far-off, in order to speak life as a possibility of the infinite. He embraced this time involving a mixture of defeats and hopes, between the temptations, shipwrecks, and new beginnings that are our existence. He embraced the silence of our impasses, of that which has been omitted in ourselves or by ourselves, the silence of this yearning indefiniteness that we are, between the already and the not yet.

"My God, my God, why have you abandoned me?" (or "My God, my God, what have you abandoned me to?" as some recent translations put it). But even in this case, Jesus' words continue to be clearly addressed to none other than God Himself. And the way in which Jesus addresses Him, calling Him "Father" and "My God," impart to the dialogue a very dense praying intimacy, making of it the murmuring of an unshakeable confidence. And, to quote the philosopher Simone Weil again: "Confidence alone can give us strength enough not to fall as a result of fear."

"Lead us not into temptation." Let us pray these words slowly, until they really do become our own. Lead us not, Lord. Lead me not, when the walls of time begin to shake, and today's words still retain the irremediable hardness of yesterday, Lead me not when I fall back, when I almost give in, doubled up and overcome by the inflexible flood that tears me apart. Leave me not alone to cross the dark and flooded corridors of uncertainty, or to lose myself in the sensation of fatigue and unbelief. Let not the dispersal of time devour everything. Let me not fall into a failure to believe in life. "Lead us not into temptation."

13

THE WOUND BEARS FRUIT
"...But Deliver Us From Evil"

As we pray the *Our Father*, we realize that Jesus' intention was to provide a model. He does not simply pray, but he teaches his disciples to pray. He produces a kind of paradigm of Christian prayer.

When we look at this prayer, we perceive that there is no debate or argument in it. One does not argue in the *Our Father*, one simply addresses everything to the Father. The vocative words with which the prayer begins, "Our Father," are clearly the key phrase. It is true that one then goes on to speak of the Father's will, of his name, of his kingdom, but our concentration is always centered on seeking the Father. We could say that, rather than asking for this need to be met or for the satisfaction of that lack, the *Our Father* asks the Father to be Father. The One to whom the prayer is addressed, the One we are addressing, proves to be the object of our petition.

Another important aspect is the fact that the first two words in the prayer are *Our Father* and the last one is *evil*. The actual rhetorical structure of the prayer says something to us about evil. If evil is what appears at the furthest possible distance from the Father, in the very last phrase, then there is a sense in which evil is the Anti-Father. It is what is most opposed to the Father.

In the last invocation in the *Our Father*, we say, "But deliver us from evil." In saying this, we are assuming that the risk of having to face evil is a real possibility. But, at the same time, we are asking that we may not be deceived in the Father, that we may know how to choose the Father at every moment and not any of the counterfeits that seek to substitute themselves for his fundamental and creative figure.

To express in words a prayer about evil is already a victory, since quite often it appears to us in the form of an insoluble problem, a place where thought and language break down. I am reminded of an essay by the Italian writer Natalia Ginzburg, entitled "Son of Man": "Some things are incurable, and though years go by, we never recover. Even if we have lamps on the tables again, vases of flowers and portraits of our loved ones, we have no more faith in such things, not since we had to abandon them in haste or hunt for them in vain among the rubble." And she goes on: "There is no peace for the son of man. Foxes and wolves have their dens, but the son of man has nowhere to lay his head." In fact, our generation is a generation of men and women who, when faced with the problem of evil, have nowhere to lay their hearts.

A DROP OF WATER FALLING INTO THE SEA

Within Judaism and Christian reflection, we have the unequivocal statement of God as Creator. All the attempts, and there have been many, to identify two competing principles in the order of creation, good and evil, God and the devil, have been rejected. Manifestly, God and God alone is the Creator. And equally manifestly, God's Creation is good. This is confirmed for us in a kind of refrain throughout the narrative contained in the first chapter of Genesis: "God saw that it was good" or, in the Septuagint version, "God saw that it was beautiful." And not only there. In the Book of Wisdom (11:24–26) we read: "For thou lovest all things that exist and hast loathing for none of the things which thou hast made, for thou wouldst not have made anything if thou hadst hated it. How would anything have endured if thou hadst not willed it? Or how would anything not called forth by thee have been preserved? Thou sparest all things, for they are thine, O Lord who lovest the living."

In the thinking that the Biblical tradition presents concerning Creation, God is Creator, the Creation is good, and God loves created life. And one cannot identify with evil the principal characteristics of the life willed by God, namely, the creaturely condition and our finitude.

We cannot interpret correctly the famous chapter 3 of the Book of Genesis without taking into consideration a whole series of subtleties:

> Now the serpent was more subtle than any other wild creature that the Lord God had made. He said to the woman, "Did God say, *You shall not eat of any tree of the garden?*" And the woman said to the serpent, "We may eat of the fruit of the trees of the garden; but God said: *You shall not eat of the fruit of the tree that is in the midst of the garden, neither shall you touch it, lest you die.*" But the serpent said to the woman, "You will not die. For God knows that when you eat of it your eyes will be opened, and you will be like God, knowing good and evil." So when the woman saw that the tree was good for food, and that it was a delight to the eyes, and that the tree was to be desired to make one wise, she took of its fruit and ate; and she also gave some to her husband, and he ate. Then the eyes of both were opened, and they knew that they were naked; and they sewed fig leaves together and made themselves aprons. (Gen 3:1–7)

When we reflect on the way the woman's mind works, we see that she is basically attracted by what is good. "So when the woman saw that the tree was good for food, and that it was a delight to the eyes, and that the tree was to be desired to make one wise, she took of its fruit and ate; and she also gave some to her husband, and he ate." If she had not thought that the fruit was good, she would not have eaten it, neither would she have given it to her companion to eat. What is the drama in this story? It is the fact of evil seeming to be confined to what is good, to be so close to it. We are standing in front of the tree of good and evil. Man operates more steadily at the level of opposites, either good or evil, but this strange mythological tree combines both polarities, the very same polarities that are in ourselves.

There is a rabbi, a cabalistic commentator named Vladimir Soloviev, who declares: "The two voices, that of God, whom we may not name, and that of the unmentionable evil, are terrifyingly like each other. The difference between the one and other is not much more than the sound of a drop of rain falling into the sea." The woman is attracted by a good thing, but a good thing that is too limited, that she plucks from the horizon of the absolute good, the greater good. It is a good for her, but it makes tragic the comparison with the statement: "God saw that it was good." God sees the goodness of things in themselves; the woman assesses this goodness in relation to herself. She saw a good that was too limited, which, by separating itself from the greater, the absolute good, becomes the cause of the experience of evil, of her sin. There is no more than a drop of rain between the woman's search for the good and the experience of evil into which she falls. But this tiny drop can attain oceanic proportions!

BUT YOU CAN OVERCOME THE EVIL

In the dramatic story of Cain and Abel, we are told that the ethical project, the fraternal project, is not an imposition by blood, as one's own blood can turn against another's. Brothers can even kill each other. But brotherhood continues to be both a decision and a project that is within the reach of human beings. They are not condemned to doing evil.

The dialogue that takes place between God and Cain in chapter 4 of Genesis is curious: "In the course of time, Cain brought to the Lord an offering of the fruit of the ground, and Abel brought of the firstlings of his flock and of their fat portions. And the Lord had regard for Abel and his offering, but for Cain and his offering he had no regard. So Cain was very angry and his countenance fell. The Lord said to Cain, 'Why are you angry, and why has your countenance fallen? If you do well, will you not be accepted? And if you do not do well, sin is couching at your door; its desire is for you, but you must/can [*timshel*] master it.'"

One of the magnificent novels by John Steinbeck, *East of Eden*, makes use of this word that God addresses to Cain: *timshel*, you can/must. The end of the first part of the novel contains a Talmudic enquiry into the meaning of this expression. The Hebrew word *timshel* is translated in most modern Bibles as "you must," but John Steinbeck, on the basis of the rabbinic argument, suggests that it should be read as "you can." And he explores this idea in some extraordinary pages. God does not say to the man who has come face to face with evil, and who is bewildered to the point of doing away with his own brother: "I will take away your freedom, I will subject you to conditions such that this does not happen again." No, what He does is to state categorically: 'But you can overcome the evil.'"

Good and evil are not inevitable, but they do constitute ethical choices. We are not confronted by a codified morality, but placed within the dynamic of a moral narrative. And we ask ourselves: "How can the dismayed Cain not kill Abel, if he is deadly envious of him, if he has a grudge, if all his rights as the eldest son have been relativized by the seemingly capricious preference of God?" Everything does in fact justify him but Cain's reasoning does not constitute a right to do away with his brother, because God addresses an unlooked-for word to him: "You can [*timshel*] overcome evil."

GETTING GOOD OUT OF EVIL

In the Book of Genesis, we have another saga, a cycle of little histories stitched together around the figure of Joseph of Egypt. Joseph gives us an eloquent example of an ethical construction as a pathway of resistance to evil. He had been left in a well by his brothers, and then sold to the Midianites who took him to Egypt. After a troubled life, he found himself raised to the position of lieutenant to Pharaoh. When he eventually met up once again with his brothers, the very ones who had sought to do away with him, it was he who helped them, because he was in a position to save their lives. The conclusion of the Joseph cycle is enlightening: "You meant evil against me; but God meant it for good, to bring it about that many people should be kept alive, as they are today" (Gen 50:20).

A whole program is contained in this brief statement. Without denying the existence of evil, there nonetheless appears the possibility of good emerging. The battle against evil is possible, and it is subject to the ultimate and unlooked-for affirmation of the divine plan. When everything appeared to be dominated by evil, in a devastating and irreparable circle, Joseph opted to affirm love and forgiveness.

How is it that evil ceases to be irreparable? When we encounter an outward appearance (a transcendence) and we transform the evil situation into the possibility of something different coming to pass, thanks to a theophany of love.

I should like here to draw attention to a page in the impressive diary of Etty Hillesum, one of the great spiritual teachers of our time.

> How is it that this stretch of heathland surrounded by barbed wire, through which so much human misery has flooded, nevertheless remains inscribed in my memory as something almost lovely? How is it that my spirit, far from being oppressed, seemed to grow lighter and brighter there? [...] And there among the barracks, full of hunted and persecuted people, I found confirmation of my love of life. [...] Will I be able to describe all that one day? So that others can feel too how lovely and worth living and just—yes, just—life really is. Perhaps one day God will give me the few simple words I need.

It is not by chance that the majority of the great figures in the Bible and in Christian tradition (we have only to think of the biography of so many of the saints) are outstanding: while not completely adjusted to the present, they live in time and also the deconstruction of time, in hope and in the emergence of the new. In this sense, they are borderline figures. This is in fact where Christian conviction is to be found: untiringly molding the possibility of hope, believing that a transformation in the Spirit can come about, will come about, is promised, indeed is imminent, and that we already live in this line of approach, that we are on the threshold.

OPENING OUR EYES

Where evil is concerned, there are so many things that we do not know, for which we have no explanation and no one can give us one. But have we any answers to the question of the good? Is it, too, not an enigma and indeed an even greater one? Let us look at the Book of Job. There is that central moment when God orders him to fasten his belt and to stand up because God is going to interrogate him. It is, in fact, a fantastic moment. Job is full of reasons, in a seemingly fully justified complaint against God, and he hears: "Gird up your loins like a man. I will question you, and you declare to me" (Job 40:7). Then God says something totally unexpected to him: "Behold, Behemoth, which I made as I made you....His bones are tubes of bronze, his limbs like bars of iron. He is the first of the works of God" (Job 40:15, 18, 19).

God is beginning his pedagogy. By ordering Job to look at the Behemoth, God is opening his eyes (our eyes). He displays before him all that is great and immense, all the things that escape us, showing him that, while there is no explanation for evil, even less so is there one for the good. There is no explanation for the marvelous work of the Creator. Love and astonishment, laughter and the day, joy and dancing: there is no explanation for any of these. Why then do we make everything depend on finding an explanation for evil, when the good is just as great a mystery, and indeed an infinitely greater one?

"Look at all the great things in front of you" is God's challenge to Job, the challenge He also addresses to ourselves. In the face of this, Job replies to the Lord as follows: "I have uttered what I did not understand....I had heard of thee by the hearing of the ear, but now my eye sees thee, therefore I despise myself and repent in dust and ashes" (42:3–6). He had heard tell of God, but now he saw God Himself. He saw the mystery of the Creator, opened his heart to his greatness, and recognized his immensity. There is a silence that is the beginning of the transformation of life.

NOTHING BUT LOVE

Paradoxical as it may seem, the experience of evil points us toward love and a gratuitous love—what else could it be? In a sense, the experience of evil produces a radical purification of all our desire for vengeance, of our need for a reward, and throws open to us the gratuitousness of a relationship. In this way, we learn to love God for God, to love Him for what He is, and not for what He gives us. In the marvelous prayer of Mother Teresa of Calcutta, we learn to thank God for the things that He takes from us:

> "...but deliver us from evil." It is curious that the verb 'deliver' which in Greek is *rhusai*, appears twice in Saint Matthew: here, in this passage of the *Our Father* (Matt 6, 13) and when Jesus is on the Cross, and so experiencing evil to the full. There, the authorities stand looking at Him and mocking Him: "He trusted in God; let God *deliver* him now if he loves him" (Matt 27, 43). The fact that this expression appears in the Gospel account in these two places is not without significance. It is as if the mystery of the Cross were the concretisation of what, in the *Our Father*, we are praying for when we say "deliver us from evil."

Apparently, and in spite of Jesus' prayer, God does not deliver him. The bystanders mock him and can do so because they witness the silence of God. The Father will deliver the Son (and all the sons and daughters) from evil, but that particular moment when the mockery was uttered is a mysterious, enigmatic moment in which Faith appears to be suspended or over-come by an abyss of silence. We know that the Cross leads on, through the Resurrection, to the full experience of Easter. But we must not forget that Jesus introduced us into a confidence in the Father, which is, above all, a way forward, the patient appren-ticeship that our heart can conjugate in hope those things that, so often, we fear are irreconcilable: the cry and the prayer.